The Passion of Jesus
in the
Gospel of Matthew

The Passion Series

Volume 1

The Passion of Jesus in the Gospel of Matthew

by

Donald Senior, C.P.

A Michael Glazier Book
THE LITURGICAL PRESS
Collegeville, Minnesota

Cover design by Lillian Brulc
The crucifix used on page 2 and the back cover by Eric Gill ©

A Michael Glazier Book published by The Liturgical Press

ISBN 0-8146-5460-6

| 3 | 4 | 5 | 6 | 7 | 8 | 9 |

CONTENTS

PREFACE

No one is a stranger to suffering. Pain touches every human being, regardless of nationality, social standing, ideology, or personal integrity. Suffering is both individual and communal. Sickness can drain a single body just as fear, violence, or poverty can waste a nation. Death comes as the ultimate suffering, bringing termination to even the most tranquil of human lives.

The struggle to understand the origin and meaning of suffering is as long as human history. It is not surprising, therefore, that the suffering and death of Jesus should have such a prominent place in the Gospels. Each of the Gospels revolves around the crucifixion of Jesus. This interest, as we shall discuss at length in the chapters that follow, was not simply in the dramatic historical fact that Jesus of Nazareth was publicly executed by crucifixion. Rather, the evangelists sought the meaning of all this, not only for Jesus' life but for all human life. How could this happen? And what purpose might it have? These were the questions that drew Christians to Jesus' death. Discovering coherence in the sufferings of Jesus might yield the meaning of suffering in their own lives.

Christians speak of the "passion" of Jesus. The subtle layers of meaning in the word help illustrate something else that is at stake here. "Passion" derives from the Latin word *patior* and it means to "suffer," "endure," "bear." When we speak of Christ's "passion" we refer, of course, to the suffering and death that he endured. But "passion" has other connotations in English. It can mean intense emotion, feeling, even commitment. People can do things "with a passion."

Both sides of the term "passion" come into play in the Gospels. Jesus of Nazareth was condemned to die; the cross was imposed on him. He was in this sense a victim of suffering and death, just as every human being is. But the other side of "passion" is present too. The crucifixion was no surprise, falling on Jesus like a tile off a roof. The Gospels make it clear that the hostility against Jesus was a result of Jesus' own mission. Because of his unyielding commitment, his "passion," Jesus put himself on a collision course with certain powerful forces in society. From this perspective Jesus' death was the outcome of his life; he "chose" death. In the language of the Gospel, he "took up the cross."

Recent Christian experience (and recent theology in its wake) has grasped in a new way these two dimensions of the cross. The cross is both what we have to endure and what we actively and deliberately take up. In the martyr churches of Latin America or China or Eastern Europe there are many Christians who continue to bear suffering as Christians do everywhere — the sick, the elderly, the dying. But in these churches in particular there are many others who "take up the cross" by risking suffering and violent death in the pursuit of justice.

The "passion of Jesus" referred to in this book implies both the passive and active dimensions of human suffering. It would be arrogant folly to suggest that what follows will solve the riddle of suffering. The passion narratives do not offer packaged answers to the questions created by human agony. But they do offer perspective and meaning. They show Jesus, Son of God and child of the universe, walking the same path of pain and death all humans walk, yet he is not broken by it. They portray this representative human, the "new Adam," displaying the many moods of the

Christian before death: anguish, lament, peaceful acceptance, stunned silence. They invite the reader to locate his or her place in the cast of characters who swirl through the drama — the hostile opponents, the betrayer, the terrorized disciples, a leader who denied, the vacillating crowd, the women who stand boldly present at the cross.

The narratives place all of this drama on the stage of biblical history. The voices of the prophets, the anguished prayers of the psalmist, and many other texts of the Hebrew Bible were drawn into the passion story to help the early church detect the pattern of God's presence, even here in what seemed the darkest moment of human history. By retelling the passion story and placing themselves in it, the early Christians found new coherence in their own passion. Through liturgy, drama, and personal reflection, generation after generation of believers have done the same.

Contemporary biblical scholarship is divided over exactly how the passion story originated.[1] In earlier decades, scholars were more confident that the passion story had enjoyed independent existence prior to the writing of the Gospels. They observed that the passion, especially from the arrest of Jesus on, was the only place in the Gospels where all four evangelists are in significant harmony. And the passion is an extended, coherent narrative, unlike the more staccato structure of the rest of the Gospel materials. The passion therefore would have been the earliest part of the Gospel tradition to take shape. Some suggested that this was prompted by the need to explain how Jesus had died and how this was in conformity with God's will and with the Hebrew Scriptures. The paradox of proclaiming as God's Son one who had been rejected by his own people and publicly executed by the Roman State (and by a means of execution usually reserved for sedition) would surely call for explanation to Jew and Gentile alike.[2]

---

[1]Cf. the discussion of J. Donahue, "From Passion Traditions to Passion Narrative," in W. Kelber (ed.), *The Passion in Mark* (Philadelphia: Fortress, 1976), 1-20.

[2]A representative of this position would be M. Dibelius in his groundbreaking work, *From Tradition to Gospel* (New York: Scribners, n. d.), 178-217. This is an English translation of a study that originally appeared in 1919.

Others suggest that the liturgy would have been the likely setting for the origin of the earliest passion narrative.[3] In a context of communal worship, perhaps even a type of vigil service commemorating the Lord's death and resurrection, the story would have been retold and blended with prayer and reflection upon the Old Testament (the Bible of the early church). This might explain the strong influence of the psalms, prophetic writings and other biblical texts on the language of the passion story.

Some recent scholars, however, have questioned the existence of any developed passion account prior to the Gospel of Mark.[4] Because the language and theology of the passion story in Mark fit so neatly into the style of the evangelist, these scholars would attribute creation of the passion story to Mark alone.

The evidence seems to call for a more moderate position. While Mark has undoubtedly shaped the passion story in his own mold and given it a new form, it is likely that the basic content and pattern of the story had been in existence prior to Mark. Given the central importance of the death of Jesus in early Christian thought and preaching, and considering the magnetism the dramatic events of the passion have for Christian imagination, it is most probable that reflection on these events began from the earliest moments of the church's existence.

The focus of this volume is the passion narrative of Matthew. While there may be grounds for speculating about a pre-Marcan passion, there can be more certitude about the sources of Matthew's passion account. The passion narratives of Mark and Matthew are remarkably similar. Both evangelists follow the same sequence of events. Matthew's account has only two scenes not found in Mark: the death of Judas (27:3-10) and the story of the setting of guards at the

[3]This was proposed by G. Bertram, *Die Leidensgeschichte und der Christuskult* (FRLANT 22; Göttingen: Vandenhoeck & Ruprecht, 1922); more recently by E. Trocmé, *The Passion as Liturgy. A Study in the Origin of the Passion in the Four Gospels* (London: SCM, 1983).

[4]Cf. the discussion of this issue in Volume 2 of this series, D. Senior, *The Passion of Jesus in the Gospel of Mark* (Wilmington: Michael Glazier, Inc., 1984), 10-11.

tomb (27:62-66; cf. also, 28:11-15).[5] A large portion of the text of Matthew is verbally identical with that of Mark.

The easiest explanation for the relationship of Matthew to Mark, and the one adopted in this study, is that Matthew used the Gospel of Mark as his primary source. The majority of biblical scholars today would support this hypothesis, even though there is persistent debate and many other hypotheses about what is called the "synoptic problem."[6] In fact, precisely because the passion narratives of Mark and Matthew are so similar over such an extensive portion of their Gospels, the passion is a very good place to test one's hypothesis about the literary relationships of the Gospels. Differences between the two evangelists, where they do occur, stand out clearly and invite analysis.

I pursued that issue in an earlier study of Matthew's passion entitled, *The Passion Narrative According to Matthew: A Redactional Study,* and concluded that indeed Matthew depended on Mark as his source, even though he retold the passion story from his own perspective.[7]

My interest in the present study is not to reexamine the question of Matthew's literary sources but to focus on his theological perspective, as he both absorbs and reinterprets the passion story provided by Mark. For Matthew, as for all the evangelists, the passion is the climax of Jesus' entire mission. Theological motifs that run through the Gospel find their resolution and most eloquent expression in the dramatic events of Jesus' death and resurrection. Because Matthew's overall theology is different from that of Mark, it

[5]However, Matthew does expand and freely alter scenes taken from his source (see, for example, 26:52-54; 27:24-25; 27:51-53, etc.).

[6]Cf. a discussion of this issue in D. Senior, *What Are They Saying about Matthew?* (New York: Paulist Press, 1983), 16-20.

[7]Cf. D. Senior, *The Passion Narrative According to Matthew: A Redactional Study* (BETL 39; Leuven: Leuven University Press, 1975.) Other notable studies of Matthew's passion narrative that would support this view include: N. A. Dahl, "Die Passionsgeschichte bei Matthäus," *New Testament Studies* (1955-56) 17-32; A. Descamps, "Rédaction et christologie dans le récit matthéen de la Passion," in M. Didier (ed.), *L'Evangile selon Matthieu: Rédaction et Theologie* (Gembloux: Duculot, 1972), 359-415; P. Benoit, *The Passion and Resurrection of Jesus Christ* (New York: Herder & Herder, 1969).

is not surprising that Matthew's portrayal of the suffering and death of Jesus departs from that of Mark, even as it depends on that earlier version.

Each evangelist tells a unique passion story (and a unique Gospel) because the experiences of each Christian community and each generation were different. The word of the cross was a living word, crying out for reinterpretation as life took new shape in each expression of the early church. Reinterpreting the Gospel was particularly compelling for Matthew's church because his Christians lived in a time of profound transition. Most scholars believe that Matthew's Gospel was written a decade or two after A.D. 70, that watershed date for the early church when Roman legions brutally suppressed the Jewish revolt in Palestine, destroying the Temple and altering forever the face of Judaism and Jewish-Christianity.

For Judaism the devastation of the war meant a profound transformation in its own life. Many of the forms of Judaism existing in Palestine prior to the revolt — the aristocratic Sadducees and the Jerusalem establishment connected with the Temple, the strict reform movement of the Essenes, the revolutionary Zealots — were now eliminated or greatly weakened. Only the Pharisees, a lay reform movement deeply zealous yet politically pragmatic, were in a position to offer leadership and unity to Judaism. Their reforms, typified by the academy of Jamnia where the law and the Scriptures were codified and reinterpreted during the latter part of the first century, would give a new face to Judaism.

At the same time, however, the Pharisees insisted on more uniformity within Jewish life and began to put pressure on fringe groups considered to be incompatible with the reforms. This eventually led to the definitive separation of church and synagogue, with the Jewish Christians being expelled from the synagogues.

This turn of events had profound consequences for Jewish Christians. Not only were they being separated from the synagogue and the religious tradition in which they had been formed and nourished, but at the same time early

Christianity was becoming increasingly Gentile in character. New peoples, non-Jewish and therefore less acquainted
with the traditions of Israel, were flooding into the Christian
communities. Inevitably these events would be a source of
consternation for the Jewish Christians who seemed to be
caught in the middle, cut off from their past and at the same
time faced with an unexpected and perhaps uninviting
future.

Matthew's church seems to have been caught up in these
kinds of tensions, and a basic purpose of his Gospel may
have been to deal with the agonies and hopes of Christians
who were astride this turning point in history.[8] As we will try
to point out in the pages that follow, the story of Jesus' own
sufferings, and his triumph over death, would have particular meaning for such Christians. The passion of Jesus was
not simply a story of suffering out of the past but a point of
identification for the Christians of Matthew's own time,
who struggled to find meaning and purpose in the cross they
now had to take up. And for us twentieth-century Christians, who also know the peculiar suffering and hope of
living in an age that is both dying and being born, the
passion of Jesus according to Matthew might have special
meaning.[9]

The purpose of the detailed examination of the passion of
Jesus in Matthew that follows is to invite the reader to
experience in a new way the power of this narrative. As such
this study is written for all those who are interested in
Scripture and willing to read it closely. Because the four

[8] More detailed discussions of the background of Matthew's church can be found
in R. Brown and J. Meier, *Antioch & Rome: New Testament Cradles of Catholic
Christianity* (New York: Paulist, 1983), 11-86; W. D. Davies, *The Setting of the
Sermon on the Mount* (New York: Cambridge University Press, 1964); D. Senior,
What Are They Saying About Matthew?, 5-15. A large majority of contemporary
scholarship situates Matthew in a community composed of both Jewish and
Gentile Christians, sometime during the eighties or nineties of the first century, in
more or less direct reaction to Pharisaic Judaism. There is less consensus about the
precise location of Matthew's church (with Antioch probably the leading con-
tender; cf. the discussion in J. Meier, *Antioch and Rome*).

[9] For provocative reflections along this line, cf. the now famous essay of K.
Rahner, "Towards a Fundamental Theological Interpretation of Vatican II,"
Theological Studies 40 (1979) 716-27.

passion narratives have a remarkable degree of similarity and yet each bears the evident trademarks of its author, they are an excellent place to use the techniques of critical scholarship in order to appreciate the distinctive theology of the evangelists. I hope, too, that the theological reflection stimulated by a close reading of the passion will be of use to those interested in issues of ministry and spirituality.

Although for the sake of a wider audience I have attempted to keep footnotes and technical terms to a minimum, my debt to contemporary biblical scholarship should be clear. Since the passion narratives have been the focus of my own research since my doctoral studies more than a decade ago, I also dare to hope that what is written here is not merely a synthesis of other interpretations but in the main represents my own reading of the text.

This volume follows the same format I will use for each study in this four-part series. An opening section shows how the passion story is prepared for in the body of Matthew's Gospel. The second and longest section is a detailed analysis of the passion narrative itself. The concluding section attempts to synthesize the theological motifs that dominate Matthew's passion and to suggest some implications for contemporary experience.

Like the beginning of Matthew's Gospel, this series has a long genealogy. My introduction to a critical study of the passion narratives began at the University of Louvain where I completed my doctoral work on the passion narrative of Matthew in 1972 under the direction of Professor Frans Neirynck. For the past ten years I have taught a course on the passion narratives at the Catholic Theological Union in Chicago. With the help of the many men and women who have taken that course I was able to see the close connection between the passion of Jesus and contemporary issues of suffering — a vital mode of biblical interpretation for which I am most grateful. The immediate stimulus for putting pen to paper was the encouragement of Michael Glazier, whose friendship and professional collaboration have been a joy to me for the past few years. I am also grateful to Professor Kenneth O'Malley, C. P., Director of Library at Catholic

Theological Union and Geneva Gorgo, O.S.F., Joyce Stemper, O.S.F., for creating the indexes and to Ann Maloney, O.P., who provided her usual great service in getting the manuscript ready for the publisher.

No influence has been more decisive for this project than the spirit of the religious community with whom I have lived and been nourished for more than twenty years. To my brother Passionists, I gratefully dedicate this work.

PART I

PREPARATION FOR
THE PASSION

Introduction

From the very beginning of Matthew's Gospel, Jesus' death looms before the reader. The atmosphere surrounding Jesus' birth is filled with threat as Herod stalks the newborn Messiah. Infants are slaughtered and the family of Jesus is forced to flee. As Jesus begins his public ministry he is tested by Satan in the desert and hears ominous news of John's imprisonment.

Throughout Jesus' ministry of teaching and healing, cold hostility by significant leaders marks every step. As Jesus leads his diciples on a journey from Galilee to Jerusalem the cross beckons like a forbidding grail. And once Jesus enters David's city and Herod's temple, the wrath of his opponents breaks its bounds. The treachery of Judas gives them the opportunity they had sought, and the long passion ordeal begins.

Thus the shadow of the cross of Jesus falls across the entire Gospel. By this means the evangelist illustrates the inner connection between Jesus' redemptive mission and the climax of that mission in the passion.[1] The death and triumph of Jesus are not an unexpected or arbitrary ending to the Gospel drama but its inner core. Exploring these preparations for the passion within the Gospel will enable us to see more clearly the theological perspective Matthew brings to his interpretation of the death of Jesus.

I. Birth Pangs

The first two chapters of Matthew's Gospel concentrate on the origin of Jesus the Messiah. This unique material serves as an overture to the Gospel as a whole, sounding motifs that will be developed within the body of the narrative. Since the death of Jesus is a crucial part of the story, it is not surprising that it, too, should have an echo in the Infancy Gospel. What is surprising, however, is the extent to which themes of rejection, death, and ultimate triumph reverberate through Matthew's opening chapters.

As we noted earlier a major concern of Matthew's Gospel is to offer perspective to a community experiencing profound and wrenching transition.[2] Matthew's Jesus is presented as firmly embedded in Israel's sacred history and tradition and yet as an explosive force that will open up the new and decisive age of salvation. For the new to take hold, something of the old must give way, even die.

This mood of historical transition is evoked in the opening lines of Matthew's Gospel. The evangelist begins his narrative with a genealogy (1:1-18) that charts Jesus'

---

[1] A number of recent studies in christology have pursued this point: see, for example, E. Schillebeeckx, *Jesus: an Experiment in Christology* (New York: Seabury, 1979), 294-319; H. Kung, *On Being a Christian* (New York: Doubleday, 1976), 319-42; W. Kasper, *Jesus the Christ* (New York: Paulist, 1976), 113-23; J. Sobrino, *Christology at the Crossroads* (Maryknoll: Orbis, 1978) 201-04; M. Hellwig, "The Central Scandal of the Cross: From Sin to Salvation," in D. Durken (ed.), *Sin, Salvation and the Spirit* (Collegeville: The Liturgical Press, 1979), 187-94.

[2] Cf. above, pp. 12-13.

Davidic ancestry while, at the same time, clearly noting the moments of unexpected discontinuity included in that sacred past.[3] Thus the tracing of Jesus' ancestry moves from remote beginnings with the patriarch Abraham (1:2) to the summit of Jewish hopes in David (1:6) but turns significantly to the apparent dashing of those hopes in exile (1:11), only to revive and reach their true zenith in the birth of the Messiah (1:16). Matthew draws the reader's attention to this turbulent movement of sacred history in verse 17; each segment of the genealogy equals fourteen generations, a number that may be a play on the name of "David" (whose Hebrew characters equal fourteen in the Jewish mode of enumeration), thereby reasserting Jesus' identity as the Davidic Messiah. Or Matthew may also be suggesting that the generations of Jesus' family tree form a series of "sevens," a number suggesting completion or fullness, indicating that God's plan comes to its realization in Jesus despite, or even through, the apparent discontinuities of history.[4]

The presence of unusual women within the genealogy also seems to play on the note of discontinuity.[5] Tamar (1:3), posing as a prostitute on the road to Timnah, uses her ingenuity to make Judah carry out his Levirate duty and to bear a son by her (see the story in Genesis 38). Rahab (1:5), a prostitute of Jericho, hides the Israelite spies at the time of the conquest and is spared destruction. Ruth (1:5), a Moab-

---

[3]On the function of the genealogy in Matthew's infancy narrative, see R. Brown, *The Birth of the Messiah: A Commentary on the Infancy Narratives in Matthew and Luke* (Garden City: Doubleday, 1977), esp. 57-95; H. Hendrickx, *The Infancy Narratives* (Manila: East Asian Pastoral Institute, 1975), 25-31; J. Meier, *The Vision of Matthew: Christ, Church and Morality in the First Gospel* (New York: Paulist, 1979), 52-56; A. Paul, *L'évangile de l'Enfance selon s. Matthieu* (lire la Bible 17; Paris: Editions du Cerf, 1968), 9-44; K. Stendahl., "'Quis et unde?'," in W. Eltester (ed.), *Judentum, Urchristentum, Kirche.* ZNWBF 26 (1960) 94-105.

[4]See a discussion of these and other interpretations of Matthew's schema for the genealogy in R. Brown, *The Birth of the Messiah,* 57-94.

[5]Biblical genealogies are patriarchal, tracing the male line. However it is not unusual that women be mentioned (see, for example, Keturah in I Chr 1:32, Timna in 1:40, Mehetabel in 1:50, Tamar in 2:4, etc.; Matthew, in fact, draws most of his genealogical material from the first three chapters of I Chronicles). The unusual aspect of Matthew is that in each case the women he mentions are "outsiders" who get into the messianic line under extraordinary circumstances.

ite, with the assistance of Naomi makes Boaz her husband. Bathsheba (1:6), the wife of Uriah, the Hittite soldier killed through David's lust, becomes the mother of Solomon.

In each of these colorful chapters of biblical history an "outsider" had entered into the ranks of God's people through unexpected, even "inappropriate," means. These moments of discontinuity, Matthew suggests, are intrinsic to Jesus' own history and prepare the reader for the most astounding discontinuity of all: Jesus' own conception. Jesus' place within the Davidic line is not insured through biological continuity (that is, through Joseph) but is an act of the Spirit who is able to cross the gap from death to life. Mary, an outsider, becomes the fifth woman of the genealogy and the one through whom the Messiah would be born. In her is fulfilled the promise made through Isaiah: "Behold a virgin shall conceive and bear a son, and his name shall be called Emmanuel." Thus Matthew dwells on the unexpected, even scandalous, aura that surrounds Jesus' conception (cf. 1:18-21).

The remarkable circumstances of Jesus' ancestry and his own conception alert the reader to the reality of disruption that will be such an important part of the Gospel story. What appears by human standards to be discontinuity, defeat, moments of scandal, and even death can through God's power become opportunities for new and astounding life. That basic statement of the paschal mystery will echo throughout the Gospel and is one of Matthew's most important reflections on the meaning of Jesus' passion. Matthew's own community was undergoing profound transformation, including the entry of "outsiders" (the Gentiles) into the ranks of his predominantly Jewish-Christian church. For many Jewish Christians these new converts must have seemed an intrusion, even a "death" to their traditional way of being Christian.[6] Early in the narrative, therefore, Matthew turns his reader's attention to the basic paradigm of Christian existence: the redemptive movement from death to life.

[6]Cf. the discussion of Matthew's milieu, above, pp. 12-13.

The threat of the cross is surely present in the circumstances that engulf the Messiah and his family as the Infancy Gospel continues. Once again the presence of "outsiders" is noted as the magi appear on the scene (2:1-12); they model the future reaction of the Gentiles to the Christian Gospel. Guided by their reverent study of nature, they come to Israel, seeking enlightenment from the Scriptures and the Jewish leaders (2:1-2). Ironically, the chief priests and scribes know exactly where the Messiah is to be born, but it is the Gentile magi who go to offer homage while Herod and "all Jerusalem" are "troubled" (2:3) by the prospect of the Messiah's birth and begin to plot his death.

The evangelist uses this material to subtly wrap the cloak of Moses around the shoulders of the infant Jesus. The coming of the magi evokes the Balaam and Balak story in the book of Numbers. Determined to destroy Moses and the people as they pursue their desert trek through his kingdom of Moab, the wicked King Balak calls on the services of a foreign sorcerer, Balaam, to curse the Israelites (see the entire story in Numbers 22-24). But finally heeding the warning of the "Angel of the Lord," Balaam refuses to curse Moses and the people, and instead confers a blessing on them.

Matthew's account of the magi seems to draw on this Old Testament story: now a new Moses and the people he will redeem are protected from the mortal threats of a wicked king and his courtiers.

Herod's brooding plot against Jesus and the brutality of his slaughter of the infants (2:16) trigger reminiscences of traditions surrounding the birth of Moses. Josephus and other ancient Jewish texts report popular legends about Moses that used the Exodus account as their starting point. The future leader of Israel is miraculously rescued from the cruelty of Pharaoh who is determined to suppress any threat to his kingdom. Now similar terrors greet the birth of Jesus. Herod's vicious attempt to destroy the newly-born king stamps the very first moments of his existence with the

[7]Cf. R. Brown, *The Birth of the Messiah*, 190-96.

threat of death. Jesus is a new Moses, and his way will be the way of the cross.

The threat does not end with the frustrated attacks of Herod. To escape the tyrant, Joseph is directed in a dream to take Jesus and his mother to Egypt (2:13). The grief over the murdered children of Bethlehem which accompanies this event explicitly ties the flight into Egypt to Israel's experience of exile. Matthew cites Jeremiah 31:15, "A voice was heard in Ramah, wailing and loud lamentation, Rachel weeping for her children; she refused to be consoled, because they were no more" (Mt 2:18). The text of Jeremiah referred to grief over the exile as the deportees passed through Ramah.[8]

Further identification with Israel's history continues. The infant Messiah and his family go to Egypt but only to be called forth once again, recapitulating the experience of exodus, the great saving event of Israel's past. A quotation from Hosea 11:1 provides Matthew's theological interpretation: "Out of Egypt have I called my son" (Mt 2:15). The angel's words to Joseph signaling the possibility of return echo those of Yahweh to Moses which indicated that Pharaoh's threat had ended and his mission of liberation could begin: "Rise, take the child and his mother, and go to the land of Israel, for those who sought the child's life are dead."[9]

Like a new people retracing the desert trek, the infant Messiah and his family leave Egypt and enter into the promised land (2:21). But the threat of death still stalks them: Herod's son Archelaus, a notoriously cruel and arbitrary ruler, now sits on his father's throne in Judea. So Joseph takes the family to Nazareth in Galilee (2:22-23). Thus Jesus enters the arena of his mission not as triumphant

---

[8] Matthew's use of this citation and its attachment to the events in Bethlehem suggest a complicated tradition history; on this point, see R. Brown, *The Birth of the Messiah*, 221-28.

[9] Compare Ex 4:19: "Go back to Egypt; for all the men who were seeking your life are dead."

claimant to his own land but as a displaced person, threatened by death.

The cross, therefore, spreads its shadow over the entire infancy narrative. From the moment of his conception Jesus is faced with misunderstanding, rejection, mortal threat. The one who carries the promise of Israel is rejected by the leaders of God's people. Only strangers seem able to grasp the moment of grace and respond accordingly. The mystery of grace and rejection is an essential ingredient of Jesus' passion, as Matthew will present it, and the infancy narrative has clearly signaled this mystery to the reader.

At the same time, the Infancy Gospel eloquently reveals the character of Matthew's Jesus. This Messiah is no potentate, insulated from the sufferings and hopes of his people. The whole history of Israel seems to be distilled and pressed into Jesus, the embodiment of God's promise. He is born in threat, driven into exile, liberated from the place of slavery, entered into a land of promise and lives in hope, not consummation. The roots of Jesus' family tree bore deep into the history of Israel, to David and Abraham. But the roots of that tree also entwine exile and other startling moments of discontinuity when Israel's life seemed hopeless were it not for the surprising initiatives of God's graciousness. For Matthew that is one of the most important meanings of Jesus' death.

II. The Destiny of John the Baptist

As in Mark's Gospel, John the Baptist prepares the way for Jesus. Matthew presents the core of John's message as identical to that of Jesus: "Repent, for the kingdom of heaven is at hand." (compare 3:2 and 4:17). At the same time, John's ancillary role is clear. He is Elijah, the prophet whose return signalled the dawn of the messianic era, an era which will explode into being through Jesus (Matthew explicitly identifies John as "Elijah" in 17:10-13; also John's garb of "camel hair, and a leather girdle" was the identifying mark of Elijah: see 2 Kings 1:8).[10] John's role is to baptize in water; Jesus will baptize with the Spirit promised for the messianic age (Mt 3:12-13). When Jesus comes to undergo the ritual of repentance, John explicitly states his subordination to Jesus: "I need to be baptized by you, and do you come to me?" (3:14).

As forerunner John's fate previews Jesus' destiny. Matthew pointedly begins his description of John's mission with a clash between the prophet and the Jewish leaders. As the Pharisees and Sadducees come for baptism, John excoriates them for failing to do the deeds of repentance — a tireless theme of Jesus' own ministry (3:7). Their claim to have "Abraham as our father" is no substitute for integrity, the true mark of membership in God's family (3:9), an inherently universal principle important for the Gentile mission and also one that will be sounded by Matthew's Jesus.[11]

The cost of John's fearless mission soon becomes clear. Jesus inaugurates his ministry in Galilee when he "hears" of John's arrest (4:17), a subtle note of Matthew's version that links Jesus with John in a more personal fashion than Mark's account (where Jesus begins his ministry "after John had been arrested"; cf. Mk 1:14).[12] In chapter 11 Matthew draws on his special source Q to further elaborate on the connection between John and Jesus. John's question from prison, "Are you he who is to come, or shall we look for another?" (11:3) prompts a review of Jesus' ministry (11:4-6) and leads into strong praise for the Baptist and his mission: John is the greatest of prophets because he is the God-appointed messenger of the Messiah (cf. the quote from Malachi 3:1, cited in Mt 11:10). Both messenger and Mes-

---

[10] Outside of the New Testament itself, evidence for this expectation of Elijah's return is not widespread. Nevertheless it does seem to have been a Jewish tradition current in the first century. See the discussion in D. Allison, Jr., "'Elijah Must Come First,'" *Journal of Biblical Literature* 103 (1984) 256-58.

[11] By stressing an ethical norm for inclusion in the people of God rather than an ethnocentric one Matthew (along with other New Testament writers) provided an important opening to the Gentiles; on this, cf. D. Senior and C. Stuhlmueller, *The Biblical Foundations for Mission* (Maryknoll: Orbis, 1983), 247-49.

[12] Note that in 3:15 Matthew had already placed John and Jesus in conversation; in Mark's account the two figures never converse at the baptism.

siah, however, suffer rejection from "this generation" (11:16-19) which like exasperated children playing in the marketplace find that neither John nor Jesus will join their games. It is the leaders, not God's messengers, who are petulantly out of step with God's call to repentance.

John suffers the death of a prophet in a macabre scene that has haunting similarities to Jesus' own fate (see 14:1-12). John's prophetic preaching had proved too much for Herodias when he had challenged the validity of her marriage to Philip, Herod Antipas' brother. John's role as prophet is admitted even by Herod, who fears to put John to death since the people revere him (14:5). But through the wiles of Herodias and the seductions of Herod's vanity, John is beheaded.

The striking parallels between the ordeal of John and the trial and death of Jesus cannot be accidental. As with John, Jesus will be delivered up because of the impact of his prophetic preaching. Fear of the multitude's reverence for Jesus causes his opponents to hesitate in the execution of their plot (cf. 21:45-46; 26:3-5), just as Herod refrained from arresting John. And the King's reluctance to execute John is not unlike Pilate's attempts to free Jesus (compare 14:9 and 27:11-26). And just as Herodias' perseverance succeeds in obtaining John's beheading, so the leaders will persuade the crowds, and ultimately Pilate, to condemn Jesus (compare 14:9-10 and 27:24-25). When John has been executed his disciples come and take his body for burial just as in Matthew's version of the burial account, Joseph of Arimathea, a "disciple" of Jesus, will claim his body from Herod (contrast Mark who describes Joseph as "a respected member of the council, who was also himself looking for the kingdom of God" 15:43).

John the Baptist takes his place among the prophetic messengers who called Israel to repentance but repeatedly suffered rejection.[13] The Matthean Jesus alluded to the fate

---

[13]On the theme of the rejected prophet in Judaism, cf. D. Aune, *Prophecy in Early Christianity and the Ancient Mediterranean World* (Grand Rapids: Wm. B. Eerdmans, 1983), 157-59; also, R. Dillon, "Easter Revelation and Mission Program in Luke 24:46-48," in D. Durken, *Sin, Salvation, and the Spirit* (Collegeville: The Liturgical Press, 1979), 248-51; D. Hill, *New Testament Prophecy* (Atlanta: John Knox, 1979), 46.

of the prophets on more than one occasion: they were the servants sent to procure the harvest of the vineyard only to be beaten, killed, and stoned (21:35-36). They were the "prophets and wise persons and scribes" whom the leaders persecuted and violently rejected (23:34).

But the Baptist was more than a link in the prophetic chain; he was the last and greatest prophet who stood on the brink of the messianic age. He had come "in the way of righteousness" (22:32) just as Jesus himself would. But even so his call to repentance had been rebuffed. The fate of John reminds the reader of the Gospel of the high price of the prophetic vocation, a vocation given its ultimate expression by Jesus himself.

III. Persecution for the Sake of Justice

Two of the beatitudes in Matthew's Gospel speak of "justice" ("justice" or "righteousness" translate the same Greek word *dikaiosune*) and the cost of justice: "Blessed are those who hunger and thirst for righteousness, for they shall be satisfied" (5:6); "Blessed are those who are persecuted for righteousness' sake, for theirs is the kingdom of heaven" (5:10). In a very true sense these beatitudes, speaking of the commitment to justice and the price of that commitment, serve as commentary on Matthew's portrayal of Jesus himself. One of the most important preparations for the passion in the Gospel is Jesus' own ministry and the conflict and hostility it stirs up.

A unique feature of Matthew's Gospel is its presentation of Jesus' entire ministry as a commitment to justice. The first words of the Matthean Jesus state the keynote of his mission. When John protests his unworthiness to baptize Jesus, Jesus answers: "Let it be so now; for thus it is fitting for us to fulfill all righteousness" (3:15). The precise meaning of the term "righteousness" or "justice" (*dikaiosune*) has been the subject of much discussion.[14] Its basic meaning seems to derive from the biblical notion of God's "justice," that is, God's faithful acts of salvation on behalf of Israel. Conversely, human "justice" refers to the totality of faithful response to God's justice; the "just" Israelite is the faithful Israelite who remains true to the covenant.

Therefore, Matthew's Gospel can refer to "justice" as something to be hungered for (that is God's justice, as in 5:6) because the believer lives by the justice of God, or as a way of life that may be costly (that is, justice as a life faithful to God, as in 5:10).

The word "fulfill" (the Greek word *plerosai*) is another key concept in Matthew's programmatic statement of 3:15. Throughout the Gospel, as we will have occasion to note, Matthew speaks of Jesus' "fulfillment" of the Scriptures. Although various shades of meaning have been suggested for the multiple uses Matthew gives this term, a basic notion seems to be that of "prophetic fulfillment," that is, Jesus brings to full expression what had previously existed as promise or potential.[15] Therefore, Jesus' life and ministry will "fulfill" all justice; that is, Jesus not only "does" justice (i.e., he is a just and faithful Israelite) but he will fully reveal what human justice entails. At the same time, the mission of Jesus will demonstrate the depths of God's own faithfulness, or "justice" to Israel. As "Emmanuel," "God-with-us" (cf. Mt. 1:23), Jesus embodies and gives ultimate expression to the love and fidelity that Yahweh lavishes on Israel. Therefore from Matthew's point of view, Jesus demonstrates the full meaning of justice.

The positive portrayal of Jesus as the fulfillment of justice

---

[14]For a fuller discussion, see B. Przybylski, *Righteousness in Matthew and His World of Thought* (Society for New Testament Studies Monograph Series 41; Cambridge: Cambridge University, 1980); J. Meier, *Law and History in Matthew's Gospel* (Analecta Biblica 71; Rome: Biblical Institute Press, 1976), 76-80.

[15]See the full discussion in J. Meier, *Law and History*, 73-81, and a more popular treatment in his book, *The Vision of Matthew*, 224-28; also B. L. Martin, "Matthew on Christ and the Law," *Theological Studies* 44 (1983) 53-70.

courses throughout Matthew's Gospel and touches every
dimension of Jesus' ministry. Jesus' interpretation of the
sacred law of Israel does not destroy that law but "fulfills" it
(5:17). The love command, which Jesus both teaches and
enacts, is the heart of the law and its ultimate criterion of
interpretation (7:12; 22:34-40). In compassion and reconciliation is found the very nature of God's justice towards
Israel (5:43-58; 18:14, 23-35).[16']

Jesus' healings ratify his interpretation of law. He acts
compassionately, subordinating the demands of the Sabbath and the laws of purity to the primary command of love
by restoring the health and beauty of God's people and by
bringing back into the community those who had been
excluded (e.g., the leper in 8:1-4, Simon's mother-in-law in
8:14-17, the demoniacs in 8:28-34, the paralytic, the tax
collector, the woman with the hemorrhage, Jairus' daughter, and two blind men in 9:1-34).[17']

He relentlessly presses his message of reconciliation: the
gift is to be left at the altar and first an alienated brother or
sister forgiven (5:23-24), the erring member of the community is not to be despised but sought out (18:10-14), injury is
to be forgiven "seventy times seven times" (18:21-22). The
disciple is to forgive as God forgives, lavishly and without
recompense (18:23-35).

But the Gospel is not utopian. Jesus' insistence on love
and forgiveness is not presented as a brand of positive
thinking or rules for etiquette. From the beginning of Jesus'
ministry it is made clear that his teaching and healing in the
cause of "justice" stand as a profound challenge to the
values and priorities that rule ordinary human exchange.
Therefore Jesus' mission of justice is viewed by his opponents as subversive and dangerous and is tenaciously re-
sisted.

It is not by accident that warnings of eventual conflict are

[16]On the function of the law in Matthew's theology, cf. the state of the question
in D. Senior, *What Are They Saying about Matthew?* (New York: Paulist, 1983),
47-55.

[17]On this, cf. B. Gerhardsson, *The Mighty Acts of Jesus according to Matthew*
(Lund: CWK Gleerup, 1979).

woven into the positive teaching of the Sermon on the Mount. The disciples are blessed "when people revile you and persecute you and utter all kinds of evil against you falsely on my account" (5:11). The disciple of Jesus is to offer no resistance to injury but, instead, to "turn the other cheek" (5:39) as a sign of the new law of love taught by Jesus.

The summit of Jesus' teaching on the law and a harbinger of the cost of that teaching is his astounding command to "love your enemies and pray for those who persecute you" (5:44).[18] Love of the enemy rather than the resort to retaliation and violence is not presented as a strategy for survival but as a response to the disciples' experience of God's own gracious and indiscriminate compassion. To love the enemy is to show that one is a son or daughter of "your Father who is in heaven for he makes his sun rise on the evil and on the good, and sends rain on the just and on the unjust" (5:45).

The juxtaposition of love and enmity found in this text is a sign of Jesus' own paradoxical mission. He would relentlessly proclaim in word and action his message of love, even to the point of death. And when his enemies would gather to strike at him, God's son rejected the way of violence and retaliation. As we will see in Matthew's passion story, Jesus explicitly refuses to take up the sword or to violently resist the threats of his opponents (cf. below 26:52-54).

The Matthean Jesus is therefore the obedient Jesus whose entire life is marked by integrity. This emphasis spans the Gospel. Jesus' own mission begins with a declaration of obedience (3:15); in the desert the Messiah turns back the seductions of Satan, reasserting his commitment to God's

---

[18]On the background of this saying and its place in Matthew's theology, cf. W. Klassen, *Love of Enemies: The Way to Peace* (Overtures to Biblical Theology; Philadelphia: Fortress, 1984); J. Piper, *'Love your Enemies': Jesus' Love Command in the Synoptic Gospels and the Early Christian Paraenesis* (SNTSMS 38; Cambridge: Cambridge University, 1979), esp. 89-99; P. Perkins, *Love Commands in the New Testament* (New York: Paulist, 1982), 27-41; L. Schottroff, "Non-Violence and the Love of One's Enemies," in R. and I. Fuller (trans.), *Essays on the Love Commandment* (Philadelphia: Fortress, 1978), 9-40; D. Senior, "Jesus' Most Scandalous Teaching," in J. Pawlikowski and D. Senior (eds.), *Biblical and Theological Reflections on the Challenge of Peace* (Wilmington: Michael Glazier, 1984), 55-69.

will (4:1-11). His instructions return again and again to this
theme: the one who teaches and does not do is the least in the
kingdom (5:18-20), only those who act not those who know
the right words enter the kingdom (7:15-23), judgment is
based on good deeds (12:33-37), the true family of Jesus are
those who hear God's words and carry them out (12:46-50),
the good son is the one who really goes into the field and not
the one who said 'yes' but did not go (21:28-32), the vineyard
is given to those who produce fruit (21:43), those blessed are
they who have oil in their lamps and act on their talents
(25:1-30), they enter the kingdom who carry out the love
command even if they do not recognize Jesus (25:31-46).

The threat of persecution, even death, would not deter the
Matthean Jesus from his pursuit of God's justice.

"THE WAY OF JUSTICE" — WAY OF THE CROSS

The "way" of the Son of Man, as the way of the Baptist,
was one of justice (cf. 21:32). That way would lead inevitably to the cross. Similar to Mark's theology, Matthew presents Jesus' ministry as moving unerringly towards
Jerusalem and the cross.[19] From chapter 16 on, when the
first of the solemn passion predictions takes place (16:21),
the narrative shifts its focus to the passion which Jesus
would undergo in Jerusalem. This journey is a highly sug-
gestive one. It is the "way" of the Son of Man who is
destined for death and resurrection. It is also the "way" the
disciple must walk in order to participate in the mission of
Jesus (16:24). Therefore the cross is no mere instrument of
death, nor is it an arbitrary ending to Jesus' life. Jesus' death
on the cross is presented as the ultimate outcome or consequence of the entire mission of the Son of God. Jesus'
outpouring of life in his ministry of teaching and healing
reaches its final moment on the cross when his very being is
poured out for the many (cf. below, 26:26-29).

The passion predictions which dominate the journey
from Galilee to Jerusalem are a critical device for interpret-

---

[19]Cf. D. Senior, *The Passion of Jesus in the Gospel of Mark* (Wilmington:
Michael Glazier, 1984), 24-30.

ing Jesus' death in this manner. Beginning at Caesarea Philippi, when Jesus questions his disciples, "Who do you say that I am?" (16:15), these detailed predictions of Jesus' passion and resurrection channel the flow of the narrative toward the culmination of Jesus' mission in Jerusalem. These sayings clarify Jesus' identity, insisting that the cross reveals the inner core of Jesus' commitment to give his life on behalf of the many. Despite the confusion of Peter and the bafflement of the rest of the disciples, that teaching is asserted with full force: "From that time Jesus began to show his disciples that he must go to Jerusalem and suffer many things from the elders and chief priests and scribes, and be killed, and on the third day be raised" (16:21).

Peter's protest (16:22-23) is vigorously rebutted by Jesus and, as occurs after each of the predictions, followed by powerful teaching on discipleship as the way of the cross. "If any would come after me, let them deny themselves and take up their cross and follow me. For whoever would save their life will lose it, and whoever loses their life for my sake will find it. For what will it profit someone, if they gain the whole world and forfeit their life? Or what shall someone give in return for their life?" (16:24-26).

The second passion prediction occurs in 17:22-23, as Jesus and the disciples "gather" in Galilee, like a troup being assembled for the ordeal ahead. "The Son of Man is to be delivered into the hands of people, and they will kill him, and he will be raised on the third day." Instead of describing another instance of blatant misunderstanding of Jesus' teaching, as in Mark's parallel (Mk 9:32-34), Matthew simply notes the disciples' "distress" (17:23) at these words and follows with the discourse on community where themes of humility, compassion, and reconciliation (18:1-35) — typical of Jesus' entire teaching in the Gospel — dominate. The location and content of this discourse after the passion prediction and on the way to Jerusalem are not accidental. This powerful portrayal of the qualities of life in the kingdom — so different from those in ordinary human society —illustrates the way of justice, a way symbolized in the cross itself.

The third prediction takes place as Jesus and the disciples are nearing Jericho, on their way to Jerusalem (20:17-19): "Behold, we are going up to Jerusalem; and the Son of Man will be delivered to the chief priests and scribes, and they will condemn him to death, and deliver him to the Gentiles to be mocked and scourged and crucified, and he will be raised on the third day." This most detailed of the predictions is immediately followed by the approach of the mother of the sons of Zebedee asking Jesus for positions of honor for James and John (20:20; note that in Mark's version James and John themselves make the request of Jesus).

This request, so out of spirit with Jesus' teaching, provokes the Gospel's most explicit teaching on the connection between the cross and discipleship. To be associated with Jesus in his kingdom means "drinking the cup," a metaphor for the death of Jesus that will reappear in the passion narrative itself (cf. 26:27-28; 26:39). Jesus' words to the brothers and to the other disciples (who become indignant at the maneuver of James and John, 20:24) continue to link discipleship and the cross but now through the issue of power. The disciples are not to imitate the "rulers of the Gentiles" who exercise their power in an oppressive way, "lording over" others (20:25). In the community of Jesus, true power and authentic greatness are expressed in life-giving service to the other. The Gospel does not call for demeaning submission; "service" must be interpreted in the light of Jesus' own mission. He is the "servant" and "slave" par excellence, active, open and responsive to the needs of others.

It is precisely here that Jesus' ministry of service and self-transcendence is translated into the language of the cross: "...the Son of Man came not to be served but to serve, and to give his life as a ransom for many" (20:28). Drawing on a saying already found in Mark (Mk 10:45), the evangelist portrays the death of Jesus in terms evocative of the Suffering Servant of Isaiah 53. Jesus, God's servant, pours out his life for the sake of Israel. Earlier in the Gospel, Matthew had already explicitly linked Jesus' ministry of compassion and healing to the Servant image. The first burst of Jesus' healing work concludes: "This was to fulfill what was spoken by the prophet Isaiah, 'he took our infirmities and bore our diseases' " (Mt 8:17, quoting Isaiah 53:4). And Jesus as the gentle, compassionate healer had evoked another reference to the Servant in 12:17-21 where Matthew quotes at length from Isaiah 42:1-4.[20]

Therefore Matthew makes it clear in the heart of his Gospel that the cross is no longer a symbol of death, nor is the crucifixion an arbitrary ending to Jesus' life. Because of Jesus' faithful pursuit of justice, the cross is the ultimate expression of his life and mission. Long before Golgotha was mounted, the Son of Man had been pouring out his life for the sake of the many. The cross was the definitive act of that life-giving mission of justice. Any disciple who wished to share in Jesus' destiny would have to walk that same way of justice and pour out his or her life in the same fashion.

In Matthew's Gospel the "cross" has various levels of meaning. For Jesus, as for the disciples who would follow him, it was interior and personal, an encounter with the mystery of suffering and death that would test his faith.[21] The opposition and the death it would bring were, in this sense, not chosen by Jesus but inflicted. Even though suffering was not sought it could lead to new life. At the same time the cross has an active, public level of meaning in Matthew's Gospel. The cross was the necessary outcome of Jesus' way of life and therefore the insignia of fidelity to his mission. As such it was "taken up" by Jesus with full deliberation.

IV. Jesus and His Opponents

The clash between the message of Jesus and the values of the world is not presented by the Gospels in the form of

---

[20]On the importance of the Servant motif in Matthew's christology, cf. B. Gerhardsson, *The Mighty Acts of Jesus according to Matthew*, 88-91; D. Hill, "Son and Servant: An Essay on Matthean Christology," *Journal for the Study of the New Testament* 6 (1980) 2-16; J. H. Neyrey, "The Thematic Use of Isaiah 42, 1-4 in Matthew 12," *Biblica* 63 (1982) 457-73.

[21]See below, pp. 132-139.

abstract theological discussion. Matthew and the other evangelists reflect on the price of the way of justice by noting the flesh and blood conflict between Jesus and his opponents.

Matthew appears to give more attention to this clash than either Mark or Luke.[22.] From the first moment of Jesus' existence he meets deadly opposition from Herod and the Jewish leaders. Conflict pursues Jesus throughout his ministry and, in Matthew's version, continues even after the death of Jesus, as his opponents seek to discredit reports of his resurrection (cf. 27:62-66; 28:11-15, material unique to Matthew's Gospel).

MATTHEW AND THE JESUS OF HISTORY

There may be several converging reasons for Matthew's concentration on Jesus' opposition. Undoubtedly Jesus of Nazareth did in fact engage in spirited debate with some of the religious leaders of Israel. Jesus' interpretation of the law, his association with people considered religiously unacceptable, and his claims to unique authority became flashpoints between himself and several of the leadership groups. Vigorous challenge to religious authority is an integral part of the biblical story, as the history of the prophets makes clear. It would be absurd to think of Jesus, himself a reverent Jew, as somehow rejecting Judaism or being anti-Jewish because of his opposition to some of the leaders. On the contrary, Jesus challenged the leaders and their viewpoint precisely because of his dedication to Israel. Therefore in reporting such conflict Matthew faithfully hands on a true picture of Jesus' prophetic role within the Israel of his day.

THE EXPERIENCE OF MATTHEW'S CHURCH

But Matthew's Gospel is not mere reporting of the history of Jesus; it also reflects the experience of the post-resurrection community, including the specific experiences of Matthew's church.

[22]This emphasis of Matthew's Gospel and its interpretation in Christian history make it important to consider the anti-semitic potential of this motif, especially in connection with the passion story. We will take this up below, cf. pp. 177-181.

From this latter vantage point the opposition to Jesus takes on additional meaning. As we have already noted above, Matthew's church was in tension with the reforms of Pharisaic Judaism in the post-70 period.[23] There is little doubt that some of the bitter edge in the arguments between Jesus and his opponents derives from this later familial strife between the synagogue and Jewish Christianity. Matthew's concentration on the Pharisees as the most consistent opponents of Jesus may also reflect the fact that these were the leaders with whom Matthew's community had the most contact.[24] Some of the specific issues that Matthew concentrates on may also reflect the kinds of charges and counter-charges that separated the Christians and Jews in Matthew's day.[25]

JESUS' OPPONENTS AND THE MEANING OF DISCIPLESHIP

But Matthew's negative image of the Jewish leaders has other functions within his narrative.[26] His sole purpose is not to pillory the Jewish leaders, past or present. In fact Matthew's Gospel was not written as a polemical weapon directed to the Jewish community but as an exhortation for Christians. One has to ask, therefore, what meaning do characters such as the scribes and Pharisees have for Mat-

[23]Cf. above, pp. 12-13.

[24]The Pharisees are the most frequently mentioned group among the opponents of Jesus in Matthew's Gospel. On Matthew's somewhat stereotyped presentation of the leaders, cf. S. van Tilborg, *The Jewish Leaders in Matthew* (Leiden: Brill, 1972).

[25]This is the important thesis of W. D. Davies, *The Setting of the Sermon on the Mount* (Cambridge: Cambridge University, 1964), who believes that the nature of the conflicts between Jesus and the Pharisees in Matthew's Gospel indicates that his community was in direct conflict with the Pharisaic reform of Jamnia. A more cautious view of our ability to know the position of the Pharisees at this period can be found in J. Neusner, *From Politics to Piety: The Emergence of Pharisaic Judaism* (Englewood Cliffs: Prentice-Hall, 1973).

[26]It should be noted that Matthew, unlike John's Gospel, refers to specific leadership groups as opposing Jesus and not the "Jews" as such. The evangelist even acknowledges the authority of the Pharisees who "sit on Moses' seat" and are, therefore, to be obeyed(see 23:1-2). In 27:25, however, he will present the "whole people" in opposition to Jesus; the only instance in the Gospel of this kind; cf. below, pp. 115-122.

thew's *Christian* readers, other than rebutting possible attacks on the validity of Christian teaching.

One of the functions of the opponents is to portray, in negative terms, the meaning of authentic discipleship. The vices of opponents are the polar opposites of the virtues of the true followers of Jesus. This is clear, for example, in Jesus' condemnation of the scribes and Pharisees in chapter 23. They are condemned for preaching and not practicing (23:3) whereas the true disciple *does* the will of God (see, for example, 7:21; 12:50; 13:23, etc.). They seek recognition and honors (23:5-7) whereas the disciple is to be humble and to seek the good of others (e.g., 20:25-28). They lust for positions of power and authority, while the community of Jesus is to be egalitarian, recognizing only one "Father" and one "rabbi" (cf. 23:8-12). They construct heavy burdens for others (23:4) whereas the yoke of Jesus and the manner in which he interprets the law is compassionate and gentle (11:28-30; 12:18-21). Their priorities are confused (23:23-24) while the disciple of Jesus has been taught that the love command must be the first principle upon which all other law depends (cf. 7:12; 5:43-48; 22:34-40).

Examples like this could be multiplied. The reader of the Gospel learns the meaning of authentic Christian existence by observing *all* the characters of the Gospel: Jesus, the disciples, the crowds, individuals who make a single dramatic appearance (such as the magi of ch. 2 or the centurion of ch. 8 or the Cananite woman of chapter 15). The various opponents of Jesus take their place, albeit a negative one, in this cast of characters. Their opposition to Jesus leads to the passion itself. Such vices, Matthew clearly asserts, have tragic consequences.

THE COST OF THE GOSPEL

Another important function of the opponents, and one directly tied to the passion, is that their opposition alerts the Christian reader to the cost of discipleship. The New Testament in general reflects a conviction that there is a profound point at which the ways of God will clash with ordinary human ways. This clash derives from the inherent opposition between life and death, between grace and sin, between a life open to others and life closed in on itself.

The implacable opposition of the leaders to Jesus' teaching and ministry is a chilling reminder of the "scandal" of the Gospel. They oppose Jesus for the most basic expressions of his mission: his forgiveness of the paralytic (9:3); his association with outcasts (9:11); his liberation of those gripped by evil (9:34); his compassionate interpretation of the law (12:2,10). An unbridgeable chasm seems to yawn between the opponents' understanding of God and religion and the understanding proclaimed by Jesus.

Matthew makes it clear that this difference is deadly. It led Herod and the Jerusalem leaders to infanticide (2:16). Early in the Gospel, the Pharisees accuse Jesus of being in league with Satan (9:34; 12:24). They reject both John and Jesus, accusing John of being possessed and Jesus of being "a glutton and a drunkard, a friend of tax collectors and sinners" (11:19). Their hostility boils over into a plot to destroy him while his ministry is still young (12:14). They lie in wait to trap him (12:10) and constantly test him (12:38; 15:2; 16:1; 19:3).

When he enters Jerusalem in triumph and carries his ministry into the temple itself (chapters 21-22) their anger seems to explode. The "chief priests and the scribes" react in anger and shock at the crowd's acclaim of Jesus and his prophetic actions in the temple (21:15-16). The chief priests and elders challenge his authority (21:23). The Priests and Pharisees, stung by his teaching, attempt to arrest him but fail because they fear the crowds (21:46). They continue their attempts to trap him (22:15, 23, 34-35), refusing to give up until finally Judas offers them a way to succeed.

Therefore the committed opposition to Jesus vividly illustrates the sharp edge of the Gospel; it reminds the Christian reader that the teaching of Jesus, even though an "easy and light" yoke (11:30), should not be thought of as placid or sure to please. The Gospel proclaimed by Jesus calls for repentance and social transformation. It cuts into the preserves of many interests and will surely exact a price from anyone who lives and teaches it.

THE REJECTION OF JESUS AS TURNING POINT

There is one other level of meaning in Matthew's presentation of the opponents of Jesus that has important bearing on the passion. In Matthew's theology the death and resurrection of Jesus stands at the center of sacred history, marking the inauguration of the new and decisive age of salvation.[27] As we will note below, the evangelist's description of the events erupting at the moment of Jesus' death are those associated with the final age (cf. below, 27:51-53); the same is true of the portents that accompany the discovery of the empty tomb (28:2-4). The earthquakes, the opening of tombs and the presence of the "Angel of the Lord" interpret Jesus' resurrection as an event of the "last days," the period of final salvation promised by God in the Hebrew Scriptures.

Matthew presents a theology of history in which a moment of death and destruction becomes, paradoxically, the opening to a new moment of life. This motif had already emerged in the first chapter of the Gospel when the messianic hopes of Israel were traced through moments of startling discontinuity and death.[28]

Therefore the decision of the leaders to reject Jesus and his message has, in Matthew's perspective, truly "historic" proportions: it is at once a moment of "death" and a moment leading to new life. This perspective is reinforced several times in the Gospel. Faced with the remarkable faith of the Gentile centurion, Jesus acclaims: "Truly, I say to you, not even in Israel have I found such faith. I tell you, many will come from east and west and sit at table with Abraham, Isaac, and Jacob in the kingdom of heaven, while the children of the kingdom will be thrown into the outer darkness; there people will weep and gnash their teeth" (Mt 8:10-12). The faith of the centurion will outshine the faithlessness of Jesus' own people.

[27]For a discussion of Matthew's view of salvation history, cf. D. Senior, *What Are They Saying About Matthew?*, 28-36. A strong proponent of the position that sees the death and resurrection as the turning point of salvation history for Matthew is J. Meier, in his article, "Salvation-History in Matthew: In Search of a Starting Point," *Catholic Biblical Quarterly* 37 (1975) 203-15.

[28]Cf. Above, pp. 18-23.

A similar motif is found in chapter 11 where Jesus pronounces woes upon the Galilean cities and compares them unfavorably with the Gentile cities of Tyre and Sidon or the perennial badlands of Sodom (11:20-24). The parable of the two sons has a similar message: the tax collectors and the harlots will enter the kingdom ahead of the Jewish leaders because they accepted the message of John and Jesus while the leaders did not repent (21:28-32). In a like vein is the parable of the wedding feast (22:1-14): the first invited guests rebuff the king's messengers, even to the point of brutalizing and killing them (22:6). Such astounding rejection brings judgment on the invitees and their places are taken by others (22:7-10).[29]

The parable of the vineyard (21:33-46) has particular importance for Matthew's salvation history perspective.[30] The parable is an allegory on the history of Israel. Isaiah had presented Yahweh's troubled care for Israel under the same allegory of the vineyard (see Isaiah 5:1-7, a text that was an obvious inspiration for the parable in the Gospel tradition). The various messengers who are sent to it probably stand for the prophets. Finally, the "son" is sent but he, too, is taken outside of the vineyard and killed (a detail special to Matthew that may refer to Jesus' crucifixion outside of Jerusalem). Mark's version of the parable had already tied its meaning to the rejection of Jesus and the turning over of the vineyard to "others" (cf. Mark 12:9). But Matthew insists on this point; he adds verse 43: "Therefore I tell you, the kingdom of God will be taken away from you and given to a nation producing the fruits of it."

This attention to the rejection of Jesus by Israel and the turning to the nations will be a significant motif of the passion story itself. Part of Matthew's concern is "moral,"

[29]It is important to note Matthew's "even-handedness" in this parable: even the newly invited guests (presumably representative of the Gentiles) are expected to wear garments appropriate for the kingdom. Thus the call to repentance — and the threat of judgment for those who ignore it — has demands for both Jew and Gentile.

[30]This parable was a centerpiece of W. Trilling's important study of Matthew's theology, *Das Wahre Israel: Studien zur Theologie des Matthäus-Evangelium* (STANT 10: München: Kösel—Verlag, 3rd rev. ed., 1964), 55-65.

that is, we are responsible for our choices: to accept God's invitation leads to life; to reject it leads to judgment (often curiously described by Matthew as being thrown outside to "weep and gnash one's teeth"; cf. 8:12; 13:42, 50; 22:13; 24:51; 25:30).

But there is also a lesson for Matthew's community in the fact that rejection of the Gospel is not ultimate defeat for God's plan of salvation. Each moment of apparent death leads to unexpected new life. Jesus' own rejection and death lead to resurrection. The relative failure of the early Christian mission to Israel meant that more energy was turned to the Gentile mission.[31] Death-resurrection, in other words, was the pattern of sacred history, in the long history of Israel and in the young history of the Christian community. It is this underlying lesson of the passion that also leads Matthew to concentrate on the tragedy of Jesus' rejection.

V. The Cross and the Community's Mission

The passion story is not simply the account of Jesus' suffering and death; it is also an account of the Christian community's encounter with the passion. Jesus is viewed in the Gospel as the representative human being. His suffering is, in a very real sense, the suffering of every human being; his triumph over death is the hope of everyone. As we shall see, the cast of characters that move with Jesus through the passion story are a constant reminder of the community's stake in his death and resurrection.[32]

We have already noted at several points the Gospel's contention that being associated with the mission of Jesus leads not only to new life but involves the price of suffering, even death. The programmatic statement of the beatitudes speaks bluntly: "Blessed are you when people revile you and persecute you and utter all kinds of evil against you falsely on my account. Rejoice and be glad, for your reward is great

[31]On this point, see D. Senior & C. Stuhlmueller, *The Biblical Foundations for Mission,* 243-47.

[32]Cf. below, Part III., 172-181.

in heaven, for so people persecuted the prophets who were before you" (5:11-12).

The price of being associated with Jesus is dramatically presented in the opening pages of Matthew's story. Joseph and Mary experience persecution, exile, displacement because of Jesus. John the Baptist, who shares Jesus' message, is imprisoned and executed.

The same costly destiny is promised the disciples. Matthew spells this out in the mission discourse of chapter 10. A saying embedded in the middle of the discourse states the basic principle: "A disciple is not above his teacher, nor a servant above his master; it is enough for the disciple to be like his teacher, and the servant like his master. If they have called the master of the house Beelzebul, how much more will they malign those of his household" (10:24-25).

This saying, linking the destiny of those who proclaim the Gospel with the destiny of Jesus, is thoroughly illustrated in the parts of the discourse which surround it.[33] As the twelve are named and sent out on mission (10:1-8) they are warned that they will be "as sheep in the midst of wolves" (10:16). They will be "delivered up" to councils, flogged in synagogues, and dragged before governors and kings "to bear testimony before them and the Gentiles" (10:17-18). Proclamation of the Gospel will also lead to divisions in families and generate hatred and persecution (10:21-23). The missionaries are encouraged to proclaim the Gospel fearlessly and openly despite threats to their lives (10:26-33). Nor should they expect that their mission will create only peace and serenity; its transforming demands will be as a "sword," setting "a man against his father, and a daughter against her mother, and a daughter-in-law against her mother-in-law; and a man's foes will be those of his own household" (10:34-36).

The reader of the Gospel can hear a familiar ring in this description of the fate of the apostle sent by Jesus. The

---

[33]On this point, cf. Radermakers, *Au fil de l'évangile selon saint Matthieu* (Heverlee-Louvain: Institut d'Etudes Théologiques, 1972), 135-138, who contends that the discourse is organized in a concentric pattern around this central saying.

ordeals promised coincide with Jesus' own passion. He, too, will be "delivered up" (*paradidomi*)[34], taken before "councils" (the same Greek word, *sunedrion*, is used to refer to the Sanhedrin in 26:59) and "governors" (the same term is used of Pilate in 27:2, 11, 14, 15, 21, 27). Jesus, too, had provoked division within his "family" (13:53-58) and would be delivered up to death by his own people. Thus Jesus' death (and triumph) are a preview of the community's passion as it bears witness to the Gospel.

The sayings that come at the conclusion of the discourse make this very explicit. Anyone who is not fully committed to Jesus is not worthy of him (10:37). "And the one who does not take his [or her] cross and follow me is not worthy of me. The one who finds his life will lose it, and he who loses his life for my sake will find it" (10:38-39).

Similar sayings occur after the passion predictions.[35]·At Caesarea Philippi Jesus had told the disciples: "If anyone would come after me, let him deny himself and take up his cross and follow me. For whoever would save his life will lose it and whoever loses his life for my sake will find it" (16:24-25). The exchange with the sons of Zebedee after the third passion prediction forcefully reminds all the disciples that sharing in Jesus' glory means sharing in his cup of suffering (20:22-23). The cross is an inevitable mark of those who seek life with Jesus.

The same message is repeated in the apocalyptic discourse of chapter 24. Following upon Jesus' climactic teaching in the Jerusalem temple, the disciples ask him about the fate of the temple and the end of the world (24:3). The discourse that follows is a forecast of the pain and victory that is the destiny of his disciples.[36]· In the midst of the crisis and

[34]The Greek verb *paradidomi* becomes almost a technical term in the Gospels for Jesus' arrest and deliverance to his opponents. Matthew uses it some fifteen times in the passion narrative alone (cf. 26:2, 15, 16, 21, 23, 24, 25, 45, 48; 27:2, 3, 4, 18, 26). It is also found in the passion predictions of 17:22 and 20:18.

[35]On this, see above, p. 30-33.

[36]For a thorough discussion of the structure and theology of Matthew's apocalyptic discourse, cf. J. Lambrecht, "The Parousia Discourse. Composition and Content in Mt. xxiv-xxv," in M. Didier (ed.), *L'Evangile selon Matthieu: Rédaction et Théologie* (Gembloux: Duculot, 1972) 309-42.

turmoil of history the community is to pursue its worldwide mission of salvation; only when the mission is complete will the end come (24:14). Once again the cost of the mission is frankly assessed: "Then they will deliver you up to tribulation and put you to death; and you will be hated by all nations for my name's sake" (Mt 24:9).

Matthew's perspective is consistent: the pattern of the cross is the pattern of Christian existence. The Gospel's view of history is neither pollyannish nor morbid. The discovery of true life and ultimate triumph over death are no less sure than the inevitability of suffering and struggle. This sober realism and quiet sense of hope emerge in some parables unique to Matthew's Gospel. In the parable of the tares, weeds are sown in the wheatfield by the "enemy"; but they cannot be torn out prematurely. Both weeds and wheat must coexist until the end (13:24-30). A similar view is presented in the parable of the net (13:47-50); the net of the kingdom gathers fish "of every kind." Only at the end will the sorting come.

In each of these parables Matthew's Gospel seems to portray a realistic view of life in the world. Both good and bad, both triumph and suffering will be part of Christian existence. Only at the end will God's judgment affirm the definitive triumph of life over death. In the meantime the disciple must be braced to expect the passion. The follower of Jesus must, therefore, be "awake" and active as history unfolds. This is the message of the parables Matthew has appended to Jesus' final discourse (see 24:36—25:46).[37] The "householder" must be alert for the night thief (24:43), the servant for the return of his master (24:45-51), the wedding party for the coming of the bridegroom (25:1-13), the servant entrusted with the talents for the return of his exacting master (25:14-30). The final parable in the series is that of the sheep and the goats (25:31-46). Those are blessed and declared worthy of the kingdom who have been actively carrying out the love command, even though unaware that

---

[37]All of this mateial has been added to his Marcan source and reflects Matthew's ethical interest.

Jesus had been present in the "least" for whom such acts of mercy were performed.[38]

As the public ministry of Jesus comes to a close, the disciples are warned to be sober and alert, waiting for the often surprising and unexpected moment — the *kairos* — when God's decisive grace will come.[39] For Jesus that moment, the *kairos*, will come in his passion (cf. below, 26:18). Matthew's consistent linking of the way of Jesus and the way of the disciple reminds the community that the same will be true in Christian experience.

Matthew's portrayal of the disciples themselves coincides with this realistic yet hopeful view of the community's destiny. Unlike Mark who tends to emphasize the disbelief and failure of Jesus' followers, Matthew gives them a "mixed" image — capable of fully confessing Jesus as the "Son of God" (14:33) yet also hesitant and fearful (14:30-31).[40] The term "little faith" which Matthew applies to the disciples (cf. 6:3; 8:26; 14:31; 16:8; 17:20) seems to best characterize his overall portrayal of Jesus' followers.[41] They do believe in

---

[38]The precise application of this parable intended by the evangelist has been the subject of much debate. Are the "least brethren" to be understood as simply the "needy" or does it refer to the missionaries of Matthew's community since in 10:42 they are referred to as the "little ones" (also in a context enjoining deeds of mercy) and in 18:15, 16, 21, members of the community are addressed as "brethren"? On this question, cf. L. Cope, "Matthew XXV, 31-46 — 'The Sheep and the Goats' Reinterpreted," *Novum Testamentum* 11 (1969), 32-44; P. Christian, *Jesus und seine geringsten Brüder: Mt. 25:31-46 redaktionsgeschichtlich untersucht* (Leipsig, 1975); J. R. Michaels, Apostolic Hardships and Righteous Gentiles. A study of Matthew 25, 31-46," *Journal of Biblical Literature* 84 (1965) 27-37; J. Lambrecht, "The Parousia Discourse."

[39]The word *kairos* is one of the Greek terms for time, and can imply "opportune" or "decisive" time. On the use of this word in Matthew, especially in reference to the endtime or final day of judgment, cf. D. Senior, *The Passion Narrative according to Matthew*, 57-62.

[40]On Mark's portrayal of the disciples, particularly in connection with the passion, cf. D. Senior, *The Passion of Jesus in the Gospel of Mark*, 148-55.

[41]On the disciples in Matthew's Gospel, cf. G. Barth, "Matthew's Understanding of the Law," in G. Bornkamm, G. Barth, H. Held (eds.), *Tradition and Interpretation in Matthew* (Philadelphia: Westminster, 1963), 105-24; J. Kingsbury, *Matthew* (Proclamation Commentaries; Philadelphia: Fortress, 1977), 78-106; D. Senior, *Matthew: A Gospel for the Church* (Chicago: Franciscan Herald Press, 1973) 53-67; J. Zumstein, *La Condition du Croyant dans L'Évangile selon Matthieu* (Orbis Biblicus et Orientalis 16; Fribourg: Editions Universitaires, 1977).

Jesus but in the face of difficulty that faith wavers. Peter's fear as he begins to walk on the churning sea is a prime example of such "little faith" (14:31). Jesus also chides him for "doubting" or "hesitating" (14:31), a term that will also be applied to some of the disciples even at the moment of the final resurrection appearance in Galilee (28:17).[42]

Matthew also makes it clear that the approaching passion causes difficulties for the disciples. Peter's reaction to the first passion prediction is presented with more force than in Mark as he attempts to silence Jesus and cries out: "God forbid, Lord! This shall never happen to you" (16:22, words not found in Mark's parallel). Jesus' second prediction causes the disciples great "distress" (17:23) and the third prediction is followed, as in Mark, by the maneuver of Zebedee's sons for positions of honor (thinly disguised as a request of their mother in Matthew's version; cf. 20:20-21; compare Mk 10:35-37).

These incidents of fear, hesitation, and little faith in the face of difficulty prepare the reader for the disciples' dismal performance in the passion story. They also reinforce the Matthean Jesus' consistent emphasis on the cost of the way of justice.

Each of the motifs we have considered illustrates that the passion of Jesus is in view from the opening scene of Matthew's story. The mystery of Jesus' passion is not the break-off point for a life full of promise but, from Matthew's perspective, is the ultimate revelation of Jesus's mission and message.

---

[42]Cf. below, the discussion of Mt. 28:16-20, pp. 155-161.

PART II
THE PASSION OF JESUS

Introduction

Matthew's account of Jesus' passion is a forceful drama that commands two full chapters of his Gospel (26:1-27:66). With sober, controlled language, the evangelist retells the events of Jesus' last hours of life. The rhythm of the narrative is fast paced. It begins with a prelude in which the passion is solemnly predicted and Jesus' opponents concoct their death plot (26:1-16). Orientation to the decisive moment of the passion continues with the events surrounding the final Passover meal (26:17-35), where Jesus interprets the meaning of his impending death.

The pace quickens in Gethsemane with Jesus' urgent prayer, followed immediately by the arrival of Judas and the mob who come for the arrest (26:36-56). Jesus is taken before the Sanhedrin where he risks condemnation by fearlessly confessing his true identity, while at the same time Peter denies his discipleship before the servants and bystanders in the courtyard (26:57-75). As Jesus is being brought to trial before Pilate we learn of Judas' tragic fate (27:1-10). The trial before the Roman governor reaches its climax as Jesus is rejected and condemned by his own people (27:11-31). There follows the crucifixion and death of Jesus, a scene of almost cosmic proportions in Matthew's account (27:32-56). The drama ends on a muted note of expectation as the crucified Messiah is buried by a disciple (27:57-61) while the leaders nervously insist that Pilate place a guard at the tomb (27:62-66).

Throughout his account Matthew stays remarkably close to what seems to be his primary source, the passion story of Mark.[1] Most of Mark's material is taken over verbatim by Matthew. However, the two passion stories are not redundant. Subtly yet forcefully Matthew retells the Marcan story, shaping it according to his own theological perspective. Throughout our commentary we can use Matthew's subtle changes of Mark as a way of pinpointing the distinctive features of his story.

Matthew's "theology," that is, the significance he gives to the death and victory of Jesus, is the primary goal of our study. The evangelist communicates that "theology" not by explicit comments but through the very telling of the awesome events of the passion. It is the manner of that "telling" on which we will concentrate.

I. Prelude: The Passion Is Announced in Word and Deed (26:1-16)

Matthew opens the passion narrative with three scenes that jolt the reader with electric contrasts. While Jesus predicts that his passion is about to begin, his opponents plot against him in secret (26:1-5). An anonymous woman prepares his body for burial, over the protests of Jesus' own disciples (26:6-13). At the same time Judas, one of the twelve, sells his master for thirty pieces of silver and sets in motion the decisive plan for Jesus' arrest (26:14-16). With quick effectiveness Matthew has introduced most of the major antagonists in the passion drama and plunged us into the riptide of its tragedy.

---

[1]As noted in the Introduction (cf. above, pp. 10-12), the relationship of Matthew to Mark in the passion narrative was the focus of my work, *The Passion Narrative according to Matthew: A Redactional Study* (BETL 38; Leuven: Leuven University Press, 1975).

[1]When Jesus had finished all these sayings, he said to his disciples, [2]"You know that after two days the Passover is coming, and the Son of Man will be delivered up to be crucified." [3]Then the chief priests and the elders of the people gathered in the palace of the high priest, who was called Caiaphas, [4]and took counsel together in order to arrest Jesus by stealth and kill him. [5]But they said, "Not during the feast, lest there be a tumult among the people."

[6]Now when Jesus was at Bethany in the house of Simon the leper, [7]a woman came up to him with an alabaster flask of very expensive ointment, and she poured it on his head as he sat at table. [8]But when the disciples saw it, they were indignant, saying, "Why this waste? [9]For this ointment might have been sold for a large sum, and given to the poor." [10]But Jesus, aware of this, said to them, "Why do you trouble the woman? For she has done a beautiful thing to me. [11]For you always have the poor with you, but you will not always have me. [12]In pouring this ointment on my body she has done it to prepare me for burial. [13]Truly, I say to you, wherever this Gospel is preached in the whole world, what she has done will be told in memory of her."

[14]Then one of the twelve, who was called Judas Iscariot, went to the chief priests [15]and said, "What will you give me if I deliver him to you?" And they paid him thirty pieces of silver. [16]And from that moment he sought an opportunity to betray him.

THE FINAL PASSION PREDICTION

Matthew begins the passion narrative in deliberate fashion. Unlike Mark where the passion starts abruptly at the end of Jesus' apocalyptic discourse (see Mk 14:1 which follows immediately upon 13:37, the end of the discourse), Matthew seems to pause and let the movement of the Gospel catch its breath. Jesus himself calmly and deliberately instructs his disciples about his impending arrest and crucifixion, appearing to give the signal allowing the final events to begin (26:1-2).

The evangelist marks the moment with an editorial phrase that has occurred five times in the Gospel: "When Jesus had finished all these sayings, he said to his disciples..." (26:1). After each of the great discourses of the Gospel a similar phrase punctuated the end of Jesus' speech and carried the reader back into the flow of the narrative.[2] The use of the phrase in 26:1 indicates that the discourse of chapters 24-25 in which Jesus had instructed the community on the future crisis and had exhorted them to remain alert and faithful was now ended.[3]

Unlike the other occurrences of this transitional sentence, however, the narrator adds here the word "*all* (these sayings)." The end is near and Jesus has finished his great ministry of teaching the disciples, which Matthew had especially illustrated throughout the Gospel by means of Jesus' major discourses. Now Jesus' teaching draws to a close; there remains only one lesson, that of his obedient death.

Through the wording of this transitional verse, the evangelist may also be subtly comparing Jesus with Moses. In the book of Deuteronomy a similar concluding remark occurs as the great leader and savior of Israel had completed his instructions to the people and was about to give them his final blessing before ascending Mount Nebo for a glimpse of the promised land (see Dt 32:45, "And when Moses had finished speaking all these words to all Israel, he said to them...."). Matthew had linked Moses and Jesus in the infancy narrative; both leaders had suffered persecution and exile at their births.[4] Now a new teacher and savior, the traits for which Moses was remembered, had completed his

---

[2]See 7:28, the end of the Sermon on the Mount; 11:1, the end of the mission discourse; 13:53, the end of the parable discourse; 19:1, the end of the community discourse. These very similar verses serve as transitional devices moving the reader from the great discourses of Jesus back into the narrative flow of the story.

[3]On the connection between the apocalyptic discoure and the passion account, cf. above, Part I, pp. 42-44.

[4]Cf. above, Part I, pp. 21-22.

teaching and was about to undergo the final act of liberation on behalf of his people.[5]˙

Jesus' words are a final prediction of the passion: "You know that after two days the Passover is coming, and the Son of Man will be delivered up to be crucified" (26:2). As in Mark's version, the passion account begins on Wednesday. Jesus' crucifixion will come on Friday, the 15th of Nisan, which that year happened to be the feast of Passover.[6] The approach of the passover was, of course, well-known to the disciples since it was a major pilgrimage feast. What presumably was known only to Jesus is that on this great feast commemorating Israel's liberation from slavery, the Son of Man would be delivered up for his people. Matthew will further exploit the connection between the Passover and the passion in Jesus' words of institution at the Passover meal (cf. below, 26:26-29).

By having the passion narrative begin with Jesus' prediction of his own arrest and crucifixion Matthew portrays Jesus as in full control of the events about to cascade over him and the disciples, thereby stressing the majesty and authority of Jesus. Since the dramatic encounter at Caesarea Philippi, Jesus had turned his disciples' reluctant attention toward this climax of his mission (see 16:21; 17:22; 20:17), foretelling his arrest, suffering, death, and ultimate triumph. This final prediction is the most succinct of all: "the Son of man will be delivered up to be crucified" — the drama about to unfold will provide the chilling details embedded in those few words.

The measured deliberation of Jesus' words are in stark contrast with the furtive confusion of his opponents (26:3-

[5]On the whole Matthew does not give a great deal of attention to the parallels between Moses and Jesus. Earlier scholars such as B. Bacon had seen this as a major concern of Matthew, with even the five discourses modeled on the Pentateuch (cf. B. Bacon, *Studies in Matthew* [London: K. Constable, 1930]). However this thesis does not have wide support in biblical scholarship today. For a fuller discussion of this question, see W.D. Davies, *The Setting of the Sermon on the Mount* (Cambridge: Cambridge University Press, 1966), 14-108.

[6]On the chronology followed by Matthew and Mark in the passion story, cf. the discussion in D. Senior, *The Passion of Jesus in the Gospel of Mark* (Wilmington: Michael Glazier, 1984), 43-44.

5). The Sanhedrin, the ruling body of Jewish leaders, gathers in the house of Caiaphas. Matthew, along with John, explicitly names the High Priest who held office from A.D. 18 to 36. Again in contrast to Mark's simple reference to an ongoing plot (cf. Mk 14:1-2), Matthew has the leaders come together in counsel. They want to arrest Jesus "by stealth" and kill him. But they do not want to do it "during the feast" of Passover less there be a riot among the people who revere Jesus.

Matthew's description of the secretive session of the leaders and their anxious plotting, as well as their intention not to carry out their plan during the feast, rings with irony and is obviously intended to be a foil to the majesty of Jesus. While he speaks openly to his disciples (cf. also below, 26:55), they huddle in secret. The Greek word *tote* ("then") and the tense of the verbs Matthew uses here suggest that the two scenes happen virtually at the same time.[7] While Jesus speaks with prophetic knowledge about the exact time of his deliverance and death, the leaders decide *not* to arrest him on the feast. As the reader soon discovers, the treachery of Judas makes an arrest on the feast possible (see 26:14-16) thereby proving Jesus' prediction true.

Thus from the outset Matthew strikes powerful contrasts between Jesus and his opponents. The Son of Man, committed to the way of justice, moves forward to the final act of fidelity to his Father. His opponents, oblivious to the moment of grace and intent on their opposition to Jesus, will become instruments of death.

BURIAL ANOINTING AT BETHANY (26:6-13)

The ripping contrasts with which the passion story begins continue as the scene now turns to Bethany, a village just east of Jerusalem, over the brow of the Mount of Olives. Here Jesus and his disciples had lodging during their stay in the Jerusalem area (see 21:17).

---

[7] On Matthew's frequent use of *tote*, cf. D. Senior, *The Passion Narrative*, 22-23.

All four evangelists report a scene similar to this. Luke's version veers sharply from the others: the anointing is not connected with the passion but is an eloquent example of Jesus' mission of forgiveness (see Lk 7:36-50). The woman who is a "sinner" anoints Jesus' feet as an act of tenderness, earning the shocked protest of Jesus' Pharisee host.

The other evangelists locate the anointing at Bethany and bring it into connection with Jesus' impending death. Matthew follows his source Mark very closely (see Mk 14:3-9), trimming, in his usual editorial style, some of Mark's colorful details (e.g., the fact that the ointment is nard; the precise sum of 300 denarii for which it might have been sold, etc.). But the substance of the story remains. While Jesus is in the house of "Simon the leper" a woman approaches Jesus with reverence (we are given no idea who Simon is, but the reader of Matthew is not likely to forget that the first great miracle of Jesus was the cure of a leper, see 8:1-4).[8] She pours an alabaster jar of expensive ointment over Jesus' head.

The act confirms what Jesus had just predicted to his disciples, for this anointing is intended as a burial anointing (26:12). Matthew's description of subsequent events bears this out: the women who will come to the tomb on Easter morning do not come to anoint Jesus' body (as in Mk 16:1) but simply to "see the grave" (Mt 28:1). This anonymous woman has performed a sacred obligation of Judaism, anointing the body of Jesus in preparation for his death and burial. Some interpreters have seen further symbolism in the fact that the oil is poured over Jesus' head. Anointing the head with oil was part of the coronation ritual of the Jewish king (see I Sm 16:12-13); does Matthew also allude to Jesus' dignity as the Messiah, "the anointed king," here?

The point of the story is not simply the act of loving service performed by the woman but also the uncompre-

---

[8]The verb used here, *proselthen*, "to approach," is used some fifty times in the Gospel of Matthew to describe the approach of people to Jesus. This is often the case in healing stories (see, for example, 8:2, 5; 9:20, 28; 17:14; 21:14). There are two notable cases in which Jesus "approaches" his disciples: in 17:7 (after the transfiguration) and 28:18 (after the resurrection). On this typical Matthean word, cf. further D. Senior, *The Passion Narrative according to Matthew*, 30-31.

hending protests of the disciples. In Mark's version it is "some" of the bystanders (Mk 14:4) who complain at the lavish act of the woman. But in Matthew the disciples themselves become indignant at what they consider a waste (26:8-9).[9] They sanctimoniously complain that the ointment "might have been sold for a large sum, and given to the poor."

Jesus strongly defends the woman. In what has become one of the New Testament's most abused texts, he reminds the disciples that they always have the poor with them but they will not always have him (26:11). The intent of this saying is obviously not that poverty is inevitable (and therefore not something to be overly concerned about) — the Gospel of Matthew, in concert with the rest of the New Testament, is clear in its commitment to justice and to almsgiving (see, for example, 6:2-4; 19:21). The point here is that the woman has done an act of love for Jesus, performing a sacred obligation of Judaism. The disciples will have many opportunities to demonstrate their concern for the poor. But the moment of the passion is here and calls for urgent response. The woman has "done a beautiful thing" to Jesus (26:10) because she alone understands that the *kairos* has come.

The scene closes with an extraordinary tribute to this unnamed woman: "Truly, I say to you, wherever this Gospel is preached in the whole world, what she has done will be told in memory of her" (26:13). In Mark's version of this saying the term used was "the Gospel" (14:9). Is Matthew's phrase "*this* Gospel" meant to refer to his own Gospel (in distinction to Mark's more general reference to Christian proclamation)? We cannot be sure. Each time Matthew uses the term "Gospel" he qualifies it in some way (e.g., in 24:14, "this Gospel of the Kingdom"). Rather than referring simply to the evangelist's own work (we cannot be sure it was called a "Gospel" at this early date) it is more likely that

---

[9]Usually it is Matthew who softens Mark's negative comments about the disciples but in this instance the reverse is true. On Matthew's overall portrayal of the disciples and its contrast with Mark, cf. above, Part I, pp. 44-45.

Matthew uses the term to mean the "good news" proclaimed through the passion story. The Greek term *euaggelion* for "Gospel" means, in fact, good news, and referred primarily to Christian proclamation of salvation.[10] Only later was it applied to the four "Gospels" as narrative presentations of that salvation message. Therefore Matthew probably understands "this Gospel" to mean the passion drama itself. In Jesus' commitment to giving his life, and in the responsive and reverent love of the woman who understands the reality of the cross, is found the essence of the Gospel. Her act of discipleship becomes an integral part of this story of salvation.

BETRAYAL BY "ONE OF THE TWELVE" (MT 26:14-16)

The course of the narrative veers sharply once again. At the very moment the woman lovingly anoints Jesus' body for burial, Judas Iscariot goes to the chief priests to barter for Jesus' betrayal (note that Matthew has appended the word *tote* to this opening verse, suggesting a close chronological link with the anointing scene).[11] The scandalous tragedy of this moment is highlighted by Matthew: the verse begins "One of the twelve..." (contrast Mark 14:10).

Matthew seems to have a special interest in the figure of Judas. Whenever the fated disciple appears in the passion story Matthew significantly inflates the material provided by Mark (i.e., here and in 26:20-25, 49-50). And he will add to the passion story the tragic account of Judas' death (cf. below, 27:3-10). Judas represents the dark side of discipleship, the potential for betrayal possible in every believer who faces crisis.

Whereas Mark simply reported the fact of Judas' collusion with the priests, Matthew presents dialogue. The end result is that now the reader knows money was one of Judas'

[10]On the background of this term, cf. G. Friedrich, "*Euaggelion*" in G. Kittel (ed.), *Theological Dictionary of the New Testament*, Vol. II, (Grand Rapids: Wm. B. Eerdmans, 1964), 721-37.

[11]On the use of *tote* in Matthew, cf. above, p. 52.

motivations for the betrayal: "What will you give me if I deliver him to you?" (26:15).

The Gospel of Matthew had clearly stated the corrupting power of wealth. Jesus had warned his disciples "not to lay up. . . treasures on earth, where moth and rust consume and where thieves break in and steal." Their treasure was to be "in heaven" because "where your treasure is, there will your heart be also" (6:19-21). In a text with particular poignancy for the story of Judas, Jesus observed, "No one can serve two masters; for either he will hate the one and love the other, or he will be devoted to the one and despise the other. You cannot serve God and mammon" (6:24). The disciples were not to be absorbed with possessions; rather they were "to seek first God's kingdom and God's righteousness" (6:34). The young man who sought to be complete went away sad when Jesus advised him to sell what he had and give to the poor, because "he had great possessions" (19:22), prompting Jesus to say, "Truly, I say to you, it will be hard for a rich man to enter the kingdom of heaven" (19:23).

Matthew suggests that Judas' absorption with money led him to abandon the one treasure worthy of his life's commitment. In exchange for Jesus he receives "thirty pieces of silver." This detail, unique to Matthew's Gospel, reinforces the mercenary nature of Judas' betrayal. It also brings into the scene an allusion to the Old Testament, the first of many in the passion story. The text referred to seems to be Zechariah 11:12: "Then I said to them, 'If it seems right to you, give me my wages; but if not, keep them.' And they weighed out as my wages thirty shekels of silver." In Zechariah's somewhat obscure allegory of the shepherds, the good shepherd is given the wages of a slave (thirty shekels of silver according to Exodus 21:32), a paltry sum which the shepherd will cast back into the temple treasury — a text Matthew will use later in the story of Judas' tragic fate (cf. below, 27:9-10).[12] Allusion to this biblical text indicates a

---

[12]Some commentators believe that Matthew intends a direct allusion to the text in Exodus 21:32 about the price of a slave, making an ironic identification of Jesus as the slave or servant. But it is much more probable that Matthew has the Zechariah text in mind.

basic conviction of the evangelist: Jesus' betrayal and ultimate death, while seeming to be the triumph of evil, are mysteriously part of God's great drama of salvation.

The agreement between Judas and the chief priests sets in motion the plan that will lead to Jesus' arrest and, ultimately, his death. Matthew notes this fateful moment with a phrase that has occurred at other key junctures in the Gospel: "from that time." As Jesus had stepped into Galilee and begun his public ministry, Matthew had noted the moment: *"from that time*, Jesus began to preach..." (4:17). At Caesarea Philippi when Jesus first predicted his passion and turned his disciples' attention toward Jerusalem and the cross, the phrase occurs once more: "*From that time*, Jesus began to show his disciples that he must go to Jerusalem and suffer many things..." (16:21). Now that Judas and the priests had sealed their bargain and the events of the passion had begun their irreversible course, the moment is again stressed. The final segment of the Gospel story is about to happen.[13]

Judas remains active in his betrayal. After leaving the priests, he "sought an opportunity to betray him" (26:16). The word used for "opportunity" is *eukairian* (a change from Mark 14:11 which states that Judas "sought how to hand him over in an opportune way"). The root of this word is *kairos*, a term meaning "opportune time" and one often used in the New Testament to refer to the endtime (see, for example, Mk 13:33, Mt 24:45) when God's decisive act of salvation would take place. In 26:18, as we shall see, Matthew has Jesus himself refer to his death as "my *kairos*" or "my opportune time." Thus, ironically, both Judas and Jesus seek the same *kairos*, the deliverance of the Son of God into the hands of sinful people. One does it to snatch up thirty pieces of silver; the other, to give his life on behalf of

---

[13]Some interpreters of Matthew consider this phrase as it occurs in 4:17 and 16:21 as signaling major divisions of the Gospel (cf. for instance, J. D. Kingsbury, *Matthew: Structure, Christology, Kingdom* [Philadelphia: Fortress, 1975], 1-25. Kingsbury does not consider the phrase in 26:16 as identical in form or function with these two earlier verses; see a discussion of this in D. Senior, *What Are They Saying about Matthew?* [New York: Paulist, 1983], 24-25).

the many. Once again the seemingly arbitrary events of the passion are gathered under the mystery of God's will.

II. *The Last Passover (26:17-35)*

Four scenes cluster around the last Passover meal that Jesus celebrates with his disciples, a segment of the narrative that gives a powerful theological interpretation to Jesus' death. As the feast approaches, Jesus, with majestic authority, directs his disciples to prepare the Passover (26:17-19). The solemn moment of the meal itself (26:26-29) is poignantly surrounded by predictions of betrayal, desertion, and denial (26:20-25; 26:30-35).

17Now on the first day of Unleavened Bread the disciples came to Jesus, saying, "Where will you have us prepare for you to eat the Passover?" 18He said, "Go into the city to a certain one, and say to him, 'The Teacher says, My time is at hand; I will keep the Passover at your house with my disciples.'" 19And the disciples did as Jesus had directed them, and they prepared the passover.

20When it was evening, he sat at table with the twelve disciples; 21and as they were eating, he said, "Truly, I say to you, one of you will betray me." 22And they were very sorrowful, and began to say to him one after another, "Is it I, Lord?" 23He answered, "He who has dipped his hand in the dish with me, will betray me. 24The Son of Man goes as it is written of him, but woe to that man by whom the Son of Man is betrayed! It would have been better for that man if he had not been born." 25Judas, who betrayed him, said, "Is it I, Master?" He said to him, "You have said so."

26Now as they were eating, Jesus took bread, and blessed, and broke it, and gave it to the disciples and said, "Take, eat; this is my body." 27And he took a cup, and when he had given thanks he gave it to them, saying, "Drink of it, all of you; [28]for this is my blood of the covenant, which is poured out for many for the forgiveness of sins. [29]I tell you I shall not drink again of this fruit of the vine until that day when I drink it new with you in my Father's kingdom."

[30]And when they had sung a hymn, they went out to the Mount of Olives. [31]Then Jesus said to them, "You will all fall away because of me this night; for it is written, 'I will strike the shepherd, and the sheep of the flock will be scattered.' [32]But after I am raised up, I will go before you to Galilee." [33]Peter declared to him, "Though they all fall away because of you, I will never fall away." [34]Jesus said to him, "Truly, I say to you, this very night, before the cock crows, you will deny me three times." [35]Peter said to him, "Even if I must die with you, I will not deny you." And so said all the disciples.

THE *KAIROS* IS AT HAND: PREPARATION FOR THE PASSOVER (26:17-19)

This brief scene sets the stage for what follows. It is the eve of Passover, the "first day of Unleavened Bread." This was a designation for the festival that coincided with Passover (already found in Mark's version, cf. 14:1, 12).[14] On Thursday Jewish households threw out all leavened bread so that they could properly celebrate the Passover (for which the bread was to be unleavened; cf. Exodus 12:15). The feast itself would not actually begin until sundown of Thursday.

Matthew has trimmed this passage to concentrate on Jesus' deliberate words and the disciples' immediate obedience. When the disciples ask where to prepare the Passover meal (which had to be eaten either in the city of Jerusalem or its immediate environs) he gives a direct command (26:18) and they do "as Jesus had directed them." There is a sense of strong authority here, much like the scene

[14]Cf. D. Senior, *The Passion of Jesus in the Gospel of Mark*, 43-44. For a popular discussion of the Passover and its role in the New Testament, cf. A. Saldarini, *Jesus and Passover* (New York: Paulist, 1984).

preparing for the great entry into the city of Jerusalem and its temple in 21:1-6.[15] By contrast Mark's version seems intended to illustrate Jesus' prophetic knowledge; the detailed description Jesus provides of the man with the water jar is found by the disciples to be exactly as Jesus had predicted (Mk 14:13-16).

The words of Jesus are of particular significance. "The teacher says, 'My time is at hand; I will keep the passover at your house with my disciples.' " (26:18). The phrase "my time is at hand" is unique to Matthew and reveals an important dimension of his theology of the passion.

The word Matthew uses for "time" is *kairos*. This term can be used in a purely neutral, chronological sense in the Gospel; in 11:25, for example, it is part of the phrase "at that time" and is merely a device for introducing a new incident in the narrative (see also 12:1; 14:1).[16]

But in most instances of the word it has a special connotation. When Jesus confronts the two demoniacs in the tombs of Gadara, they cry out: "What have you to do with us, O Son of God? Have you come here to torment us before the *time* (*kairos*)?" Here the word *kairos* seems equivalent to the endtime, or the Day of the Lord, when God's salvation would sweep away all evil. *Kairos* has a similar meaning in Matthew's parable of the tares where the householder speaks of the "harvest time" when the weeds and wheat will be separated (13:30). Jesus later explains this allegory and defines the harvest time as "the close of the age" (13:40).

The association of *kairos* with the final age when God would consummate all history and bring definitive salvation to the world gives the word its special theological weight. This special meaning seems to be at work when Jesus uses the word to refer to his approching death in 26:18. Even the term "draw near" (*eggus* in Greek) is repeatedly used in the

---

[15]The pattern of a solemn command and prompt, formal obedience in both these scenes is found frequently in the Bible; on this, cf. R. Pesch, "Eine alttestamentliche Ausführungsformel im Matthäus-Evangelium. Redaktionsgeschichtliche und exegetische Beobachtungen," *Biblische Zeitschrift* 10 (1966) 220-45; 11 (1967) 79-95.

[16]On this word, cf. above, 26:16 and Part I, p. 44.

New Testament to describe the "approach" of the final age of history.[17] As Matthew will make clear later in the narrative (cf. 27:51-53) the death of Jesus was indeed the turning point of history, the breakthrough of the New Age of salvation. Because of its decisive character it anticipates the final moment of history when human destiny is determined.

As this awesome moment closes in on Jesus, he chooses to celebrate a final Passover meal with his disciples. Some scholars have questioned whether the meal described in 26:26-29 was actually a Passover meal since some of the characteristic features of the Passover celebration are not mentioned.[18] Whatever the actual historical circumstances of the final meal of Jesus and his disciples, it is clear that Matthew (following Mark) considers this to be a *Passover* celebration. The rich symbolism of that liberation celebration is used to interpret the meaning of Jesus' death and resurrection.

The formulation of Jesus' statement rings with determination: "I will keep the Passover at your house with my disciples." (26:18) Emphasis also falls on "with my disciples." That bond between Jesus and his followers will soon be under assault, as the following scene makes clear.

"ONE OF YOU WILL BETRAY ME" (26:20-25)

It is after sundown and the feast of Passover has begun (26:20). Jesus and his twelve disciples come into the city to celebrate the Passover meal as planned. But the passion story immediately introduces a poignant note into the celebration. While they are eating, Jesus predicts "one of you will betray me" (26:21).

[17]In Matthew 21:34 the verb is used to describe the fateful harvest, an obvious allegory for the endtime; in 26:45-46 it will be applied to the approach of the "hour" and of the "betrayer" — both moments having eschatological connotations for Matthew (cf. our discussion of these texts below). For further details on this verb in the New Testament, cf. H. Preisker, "*eggizo*," G. Kittel (ed.), *Theological Dictionary of the New Testament*. Vol. II, 330-32.

[18]On this, cf. J. Jeremias, *The Eucharistic Words of Jesus* (New York: Scribners, rev. ed. 1966), 15-88; I. H. Marshall, *Last Supper and Lord's Supper* (Grand Rapids: Wm. B. Eerdmans, 1980), 57-75. After reviewing the evidence both authors conclude that the last supper was in fact a Passover meal.

Matthew designs this scene so that it mounts in tension until the confrontation between Jesus and Judas in verse 25. When the disciples first hear Jesus' chilling prediction, they are stabbed with fear and begin to ask the troubled question: "It is not I, is it, Lord?" (26:22). The passage is calculated to draw the Christian reader into the story to ask the same question.

Matthew adds the title "Lord" to Mark's version of the question (compare Mk 14:19). This is an important title in Matthew's Gospel, occurring more frequently in this Gospel than in any other.[19] The title emphasizes the authority of Jesus and the divine power at work in him; it is often used in the healing stories (e.g., 8:2) or in moments of crisis (e.g., Mt. 8:25; 14:30) to express confident faith in Jesus. By placing this title on the lips of the disciples, Matthew emphasizes their faith and puts their troubled but sincere question in bold contrast to the words of Judas in verse 25.

Jesus' reply (26:23) tightens the net around the guilty Judas: "He who has dipped his hand in the dish with me will betray me." The meal setting and the prophetic words of Jesus emphasize the tragedy of Judas' betrayal — he violates the very bond of friendship and trust which Jesus celebrates with his disciples. It is the ultimate Christian sin and one that Jesus laments in verse 24: "Woe to that man by whom the Son of Man is betrayed! It would have been better for that man if he had not been born." Two deep currents of the passion tradition and Matthew's own theology merge here. On the one hand, the death of Jesus is not an accident nor an absurd tragedy resulting from Judas' sin. "The Son of Man goes as it is written of him." From the first moment of Jesus' existence God's loving providence had directed him to "fulfill all justice" (3:15), to faithfully carry out the work of salvation promised in the Scriptures and now entrusted to God's son. Nothing could deter him from that, neither the enticements of Satan (4:1-11), nor the hostility of

---

[19] The title occurs 79 times in the Gospel of Matthew (compared to 17 occurrences in Mark and Luke respectively). In many instances it is applied to Jesus in contexts asserting his authority and power. On this cf. F. Hahn, *The Titles of Jesus in Christology* (London: Lutterworth Press, 1969), 68-128; R. Fuller, *The Foundations of New Testament Christology* (New York: Scribner, 1965), 184-185.

his opponents, nor the blow of friendship betrayal, not even death itself.

But neither is Judas a helpless marionette. Jesus addresses a prophet's "woe" to him because Judas, too, is a responsible child of God and must bear the consequences of his choice. Throughout his Gospel Matthew has stressed the theme of "judgment."[20] We are responsible for our decisions: to reject the Gospel and to choose silver would lead Judas to a terrible fate.

The commitment of Judas to evil is sealed by his question: "It is not I, is it, Rabbi?" (26:25). These words are found only in Matthew, evidence of his special interest in this lost disciple. The question is identical to that of the disciples earlier, with one important difference: instead of calling Jesus "Lord," Judas addresses him as "Rabbi." In Matthew's Gospel this term seems to take on negative connotations, perhaps stemming from the hostility between the synagogue and Matthew's community.[21] Judas will greet Jesus again with this title in Gethsemane as he plants his treacherous kiss, the signal for the arrest (26:49). In Jesus' strong denunciation of the scribes and Pharisees in the discourse of chapter 23 he had skewered them for "loving [to receive]. . . salutations in the market place, and being called Rabbi by people" (23:7). The disciples were warned *not* to be called "Rabbi" because they have only one teacher (*didaskalos*) and that is Jesus himself (23:8). On three other occasions when someone calls Jesus "Rabbi" in Mark's account, Matthew chooses some other title or designation in his parallel.[22]

[20]Emphasis on judgment seems to come at the end of practically every discourse of Jesus in Matthew's Gospel: e.g., 7:21-27; 10:32-42; 13:40-43, 49-50; 18:32-35; and throughout the discourse of chs. 24-25. On this motif in Matthew, cf. D. Marguerat, *Le Jugement dans l'Evangile de Matthieu* (Geneva: Labor et Fides, 1981).

[21]Cf. above, pp. 34-35.

[22]In Mark's Gospel Peter twice addresses Jesus as "Rabbi" and both times Matthew changes it: at the transfiguration "Rabbi" (Mk 9:5) becomes "Lord" (Mt 17:4), and Peter again uses "Rabbi" when he discovers the fig tree withered (Mk 11:21), an address omitted by Matthew (Mt 21:20). In Mk 10:51 Bartimaeus addresses Jesus as "Rabbi" and this is changed to "Lord" in Matthew's version of the story (Mt 20:33).

By addressing Jesus as "Rabbi" Matthew indicates that Judas speaks as do the enemies of Jesus, failing to perceive his master's true identity. His failure is not only a result of avarice but stems from broken faith.

Judas' question was intended to deflect the glare of Jesus' accusing words. But the truth implied in his question is confirmed by Jesus' response: "You have said so" (26:25) — Judas' own words condemn him. The same response on Jesus' part is found in 26:64 where the High Priest's key question, "Are you the Christ, the son of God?" is similarly confirmed by Jesus' "You have said so." Likewise Pilate's "Are you the king of the Jews?" is answered by Jesus, "You have said so" (27:11). In each case the questioner has stated the truth in question form; Jesus' reply confirms that truth.

Judas' words unwittingly reveal his commitment to destroy Jesus and thereby to dissolve the core meaning of his own life.

THE FINAL PASSOVER: THE BODY BROKEN...THE BLOOD POURED OUT (26:26-29)

Jesus' actions and words at the Passover meal are the heart of this section of the passion narrative. Matthew follows the text of Mark very closely. Most of the changes he does make in the text of his source are the kind of stylistic ones Matthew is in the habit of doing throughout his Gospel.[23] Perhaps the most visible change is a balance between the words over the bread and the words over the cup. The command to "eat" is introduced in 26:26 (contrast Mk 14:22) paralleling the command to "drink" in 26:27.[24] Where

[23]Some commentators attribute Matthew's alterations of Mark in this scene to "liturgical" influence (see, for example, J. Jeremias, *The Eucharistic Words of Jesus*, 97). However, most of the changes Matthew has introduced are typical of his style and his reactions to Mark's account throughout the Gospel and need not be the result of liturgical influence; on this cf. D. Senior, *The Passion Narrative according to Matthew*, 76-88.

[24]Replacing indirect discourse with direct is typical of Matthew's style throughout his gospel; see in the passion narrative, for example, 26:2 (compare Mk 14:1), 26:39 (compare Mk 14:35b), 26:42 (compare Mk 14:39). For further discussion of this aspect of Matthew's style, cf. D. Senior, *The Passion Narrative*, 17-18.

Mark presupposes the command to drink from the cup, Matthew expressly states it (compare Mt 26:27 with Mk 14:23). Other changes, however, reflect Matthew's own theological perspective; these we will examine in more detail.

For both Mark and Matthew the so-called "institution" account serves as a profound statement about the meaning of Jesus' death. During the meal Jesus takes bread, blesses it, breaks and distributes it to the disciples, inviting them to eat of it. He also blesses and distributes the cup.

Those ritual gestures immediately recall the two great feeding stories earlier in the Gospel, one in Jewish territory and one among Gentiles, where Jesus had taken a small amount of provisions and miraculously fed the multitudes (see 14:13-21; 15:32-39). The significance of these two stories are an important starting point for understanding the meaning of the last supper.

In both instances the miraculous feedings draw on a rich background of biblical symbolism. Both feedings take place in the "wilderness" (Mt 14:13, 15; 15:33), recalling God's miraculous feeding of the people with the manna during their exodus through the desert (cf. Exodus 16). Multiplying food for those in need also triggers the biblical memory of the great prophet Elijah who miraculously increased the supply of meal and oil for a starving widow of Zrephath and her son (I Kings 17) and the great miracle of his successor Elisha who fed a hundred men on twenty loaves of barley and a few ears of grain (2 Kgs 4:42-44).

The feedings not only recall great saving actions of the past but are symbolic of future hope. One of Israel's ways of dreaming of future salvation was through the symbol of a great meal that God would spread on Sion, where choice wine and rich meat would be in abundance (see, for example Is 26:6-9).

The double feedings, for Jews and Gentiles, in Matthew's Gospel express the very intent of Jesus' messianic mission.[25]

---

[25]On the universalism inherent in having two feedings, one for Jews and the other for Gentiles, cf. D. Senior, "The Eucharist in Mark: Mission, Reconciliation, Hope," *Biblical Theology Bulletin 12* (1982) 67-72.

Jesus had gathered and fed God's people throughout his ministry, not only by the loaves but through his powerful word and his healing touch, through his solidarity with outcasts and his compassionate interpretation of law. In each case Jesus was driven by compassion for God's people. That is what triggers the first burst of his healing activity (cf. Mt 4:23-5:1) and what leads him to call disciples to share in his messianic work (9:36-38). Compassion, Matthew explicitly notes, is what leads Jesus to feed the multitudes (14:14; 15:32). For this reason the feeding stories are most representative of the intent and scope of Jesus' ministry.

The last supper brings the spirit of the feeding stories into explicit connection with the death of Jesus and gives that death its true meaning. It is the passover, the great feast commemorating Israel's liberation. The people about to be freed from slavery eat a meal in haste, an event the Jewish people would not forget. At the Passover meal which celebrated that redemptive moment, Jesus again takes food, blesses, breaks, and distributes it. But his words bring a new depth of meaning to the loaves and the cup. The disciples are told to take and eat for "this is my body" (26:26). They are to drink of the cup "for this is my blood of the covenant which is poured out for the many for the forgiveness of sins" (26:28). The broken loaf is declared to be the broken body of Jesus and the cup shared among the disciples is his blood poured out. The ritual gesture of Jesus states the reality of his impending death.

That death takes on meaning from the very spirit of Jesus' entire life. The words interpreting the cup are most explicit. The cup had already been used as a symbol of Jesus' death in the discussion with Zebedee's sons ("Are you able to drink the cup that I am to drink?" 20:22) and would be so used again in Gethsemane (cf. below 26:39).

The cup contains "the blood of the covenant." The words are most probably drawn from Exodus 24 which narrates the ratifying of the covenant between Yahweh and Israel. Moses takes the blood of a slaughtered ox and splashes some on the altar and some on the people. Blood was considered the source of life and Moses' action symbolizes the bond of life now binding God and the people: "Behold *the blood of the covenant* which the Lord has made with you in accordance with all these words" (Ex 24:8). For their part the people proclaim their loyalty to God and the covenant: "All that the Lord has spoken we will do, and we will be obedient" (Ex 24:7).

Matthew sees this covenant renewed and embodied in Jesus himself.[26] He becomes the living blood bond between God and God's people. That notion of Jesus as the living covenant was already stated at the beginning of the Gospel; the name given to Jesus is "Emmanuel," "God-with-us" (1:23). Throughout the Gospel the bond between Jesus and God's people is affirmed. Wherever two or three are gathered, the living Christ is there in the midst of them (18:20). In his final meeting with the disciples, the Risen Christ would promise his abiding presence with his church until the end of time (28:20). That covenant bond was especially present with the lowly and the despised. A cup of water given to a "little one" is given to Jesus who is in solidarity with them (Mt 10:42); an act of compassion or hospitality offered to "the least" is thereby done to Jesus who is bound to them (25:31-46).

Covenant, therefore, becomes for Matthew's Gospel an important symbol for redemption. By giving his body-person in love for his people, Jesus forges with them a new covenant of salvation, a covenant in which the disciples are to participate — eating of the bread, drinking of the cup. An incredible, indelible bond is forged between the altar and the people, rivaling the blood bond of Sinai.

Other biblical allusions enrich the extraordinary words over the cup. The blood of the covenant is poured out "for the many." This phrase is found in Mark's text, too, but Matthew uses the preposition *peri* in place of Mark's *huper*.

[26]Some early manuscripts read "my blood of the *new* covenant." This would suggest the influence of Jeremiah 31:31-34 who speaks of a "new covenant" being established in the final age of salvation. Whether or not Matthew explicitly alludes to the text he certainly sees Jesus' death as the establishment of the new and definitive covenant with God. This aspect of Matthew's theology is stressed by H. Frankemoelle in his work, *Jahwebund und Kirche Christi* (Neutestamentliche Abhandlungen n.f. 10; Münster: Aschendorff, 1973).

Both words mean "for" but Matthew's choice is identical with the word used in the Septuagint to translate Isaiah 53:4, 10 where the Servant is described as atoning for the sins of the many ("many" is a semitic expression that is inclusive, equivalent to "all" in English). Thus Matthew highlights the allusion to the Suffering Servant.

Jesus as the Servant of God who atones for the sins of the people is an important part of Matthew's christology. One of the names given to the infant Messiah is "Jesus" (literally, "God's help" or "God's salvation"), a name the Angel of the Lord interprets as designating Jesus' messianic mission: "for he will save his people from their sins" (1:21)[27] As God's Servant Jesus liberates his people by bearing away their burdens and healing them. In 8:17 after Jesus' first burst of healing activity, Matthew uses Is 53:4 to describe Jesus as the Servant of God: "This was to fulfill what was spoken by the prophet Isaiah, 'He took our infirmities and bore our diseases.'" Another Servant text (Is 42:1-4) is applied to Jesus later in the Gospel, again in connection with his healing:

> "Behold, my servant whom I have chosen, my beloved with whom my soul is well pleased. I will put my Spirit upon him, and he shall proclaim justice to the Gentiles. He will not wrangle or cry aloud, nor will anyone hear his voice in the streets; he will not break a bruised reed or quench a smoldering wick, till he brings justice to victory; and in his name will the Gentiles hope" (Mt 12:17-21).[28]

A key text that links the Servant image with Jesus' death is found in 20:28, at the conclusion of Jesus' instruction on

[27] Matthew uses the name Jesus much more frequently than the other evangelists (154 times compared to 80 in Mark). In the passion narrative he frequently substitutes the name Jesus for Mark's indefinite pronoun; on this, cf. D. Senior, *The Passion Narrative*, 25-26.

[28] This text refers primarily to Jesus' humility and gentleness but the last verse of the quote relates it to the redemptive work of Jesus: "till he brings justice to victory; and in his name will the Gentiles hope." Immediately before introducing the quote Matthew had summarized Jesus' healing activity (cf. Mt 12:15). On the role of Servant typology in Matthew's Gospel cf. above, Part I, pp. 32-33.

discipleship, following the final passion prediction on the road to Jerusalem. Jesus' own commitment to serve becomes the model for authentic discipleship. That service comes to its ultimate expression in the death of Jesus: "...even as the Son of Man came not to be served but to serve, and to give his life as a ransom for many."[29] Jesus' entire life was not a quest for self-aggrandizement but a pouring out of life on behalf of others. That commitment to life comes to its fullest and most effective expression in Jesus' death "for the many."

To Jesus' words over the cup Matthew alone adds the phrase, "for the forgiveness of sins" (26:29; contrast Mk 14:24). Here, too, the full significance of Jesus' redemptive mission is expressed. Matthew takes care to reserve the power of forgiving sin to Jesus. Mark had described John as preaching "a baptism of repentance for the forgiveness of sins" (Mk 1:4), but in Matthew John's message is simply: "Repent, for the kingdom of heaven is at hand." (3:2). The one who bears the name "Jesus" is the one who will lift away the burden of sin (1:21). That is the object of Jesus' urgent commitment to heal, soothing broken bodies and broken spirits. That power is challenged when Jesus declares the sins of the paralytic forgiven but his response is firm: "...that you may know that the Son of Man has authority on earth to forgive sins" (Mt 9:6). Reconciliation and forgiveness become the hallmark of the Matthean Jesus (see, for example, 5:23-24; 6:12, 14-15; 18:21-35).

The words over the cup affirm that Jesus' death is the ultimate redeeming act, the true Passover event, liberating humanity from the radical power of sin. Matthew will dramatically portray that conviction at the moment of Jesus' death when the tombs are split open and those asleep in death are freed (see below, 27:51-53). The biblical world viewed sin and death as allies; by breaking the power of death Jesus had loosened evil's grip on creation.

---

[29] In this instance Matthew uses the preposition *anti*, the same as his source Mark (cf. Mk 10:45). This text is not a direct quotation from Isaiah 53 but seems to draw on Isaiah's overall portrayal of the servant of Israel.

This extraordinary supper scene closes with a fierce promise of hope. Jesus solemnly tells the disciples: "From this moment on I shall not drink again of the fruit of the vine until that day when I drink it new with you in my Father's kingdom" (26:29). This remarkable promise is also found in Mark's Gospel. It smacks of Jesus' own language. There is a clear recognition of impending death ("I shall not drink again of the fruit of the vine. . . .") but also an unflinching challenge of hope cast into that yawning darkness: "until that day when I drink it with you in my Father's Kingdom."

Jesus' words are, in effect, another prediction of his passion and resurrection but unlike most of the others in the Gospel there is no hint here of the actual circumstances of Jesus' death or vindication. It uses classical images of the biblical tradition: "drinking of the fruit of the vine," sharing in the "kingdom" of God. For these reasons some scholars believe this is a most authentic saying of Jesus, one whose wording has been little influenced by reminiscence of the actual events of the passion and resurrection.[30]

Matthew's version of the saying contains some minor changes that subtly express the viewpoint of his Gospel. He adds the phrase, "from this moment on" (*ap'arti*), which intensifies Jesus' awareness of the impending moment (similar to the saying about the approach of the *kairos* in 26:18). And he includes the words "with you" in Jesus' triumphant assertion of hope. The disciples who ate and drank Passover with Jesus on the night of his passion will eat and drink with him again in the glory of the kingdom of his Father.[31]

The gestures and words of Jesus at the final Passover meal are, therefore, a profound statement about the meaning of Jesus' death, one drenched in biblical symbolism. His death would be the final expression of his entire life and

[30]On this cf. R. Pesch, *Das Abendmahl und Jesu Tödesverstandnis* (Quaestiones Disputatae 80; Friburg: Herder & Herder, 1978; and I. H. Marshall, *Last Supper and Lord's Supper*, 53-56.

[31]Note that Matthew's expression "Father's kingdom" is also typical of the evangelist's style; in 13:43 he refers to the "kingdom of their father" and he frequently alters Mark's formulation "kingdom of *God.*" On this cf. D. Senior, *The Passion Narrative*, 86.

mission: it was a body broken and given, it was a cup poured out, to be taken and consumed. It was a life of service for the other, a renewed covenant between God and God's people, a pledge of freedom. It was an act of gracious forgiveness. It was, finally, a real encounter with the terror of death but one that would end not with defeat but with wine drunk in the kingdom of God.

YOU WILL ALL FALL AWAY BECAUSE OF ME (MT. 26:30-35)

This scene completes the frame of discipleship failure that poignantly surrounds the last supper. Just as Jesus had predicted the betrayal of Judas so now he foretells the denial of Peter and the flight of all the disciples. Except for a number of stylistic changes Matthew's account is practically identical with that of Mark.

The Passover meal traditionally concluded with the singing of the "Hallel" (Ps 114-118). As Jesus and his disciples leave the supper room they sing these triumphant psalms that acclaim God's redemptive power and his faithfulness to Israel in its struggle for freedom. Precisely at this moment Jesus shatters the festive mood by speaking of the disciples' flight: "You will all fall away because of me [literally: "be scandalized in me"] this night..." (26:31).

Matthew's text includes the emphatic words "in me" (contrast Mk 14:27). Jesus himself and his commitment to the kingdom will become the scandal or "stumbling block" for the disciples. When they realize that following him does indeed mean the way of the cross they will flee from him. Experiencing Jesus as a "scandal" or "stumbling block" has already been acknowledged in Matthew's Gospel. When messengers from John come inquiring about Jesus, he declares: "Blessed is the one who takes no offense at me" [literally, one who is not "scandalized in me"] (11:6). His own clan in Nazareth who were stunned by his mighty works also "took offense at him" (13:57). And Jesus' declaration that it is not what goes into someone that defiles them but what comes out of their heart causes the Pharisees to "take offense" (15:12). Throughout the Gospel, therefore, Jesus was a "scandal," causing offense and shattering the persepectives of those looking for another Messiah and another way.

Now it was the turn of Jesus' own disciples to trip over the stumbling block. Their flight would fulfill the words of Zechariah 13:7: "I will strike the shepherd, and the sheep of the flock will be scattered" (Mt. 26:31). Matthew had portrayed Jesus as the true shepherd of Israel because of his compassion for the helpless and scattered crowds (see 9:36); that same compassion had led to the feeding of the multitudes (15:24). But now the flock he had gathered together would be scattered by the power of death. Following upon the "death" of the community would come resurrection: "But after I am raised up, I will go before you to Galilee" (26:32). This is the first time in the passion narrative that explicit resurrection vocabulary has been used. Jesus promises to go ahead of his disciples to Galilee, the place where they had first been gathered (4:18-22) and empowered for their mission (10:1-42). There the wounds of failure would be healed and the disciples renewed in their mission. Matthew will narrate these beautiful moments of reconciliation and recommission in 28:16-20, when Jesus gathers with his disciples on a mountaintop in Galilee. [32]

It is important to note that this text uses the language of death and resurrection to speak of the scattering and regrouping of the community. This was a genuine "passion," just as real as the physical death and resurrection that Jesus would experience and which he had spoken of in other terms during the supper (see 26:29).[33] It was undoubtedly important for the shattered Matthean community to recall these words of Jesus.

The promise of eventual reconciliation between Jesus and the disciples is a word of hope in the darkness, but the darkness still envelops the passion account. Those shadows close in again with Peter's defiant bravado: "Though they all

[32]Cf. below, pp. 155-161.

[33]On the passion of the community, cf. above, Part I, pp. 40-45.

fall away because of you, I will never fall away" (26:33); his words directly contradict Jesus' own prediction. To the parallel in Mark's account Matthew adds the words "because of you (as in the prediction of Jesus in verse 31) — the bond between Jesus and his disciples, already so strongly emphasized at the supper (see 26:29 "with you"), is ironically reaffirmed by Peter.

Jesus repeats his prediction of the apostle's denial, adding the specific moment when it would occur, "this very night, before the cock crows" (26:34), and the number of times ("three") Peter would deny him.[34] Peter stubbornly holds his ground: "Even if I must die with you, I will not deny you." His vain confidence seems to infect the other disciples who all declare the same thing (26:35).

Matthew gives special attention to Peter in his Gospel.[35] Texts such as the walking on the water in 14:28-31, the lavish blessing of Peter in 16:16-19, and Peter's role as spokesman for Jesus in the matter of the half-shekel tax in 17:24-27 are materials found only in Matthew's Gospel. In each instance it is interesting to note that Matthew both extols and sharply criticizes the Apostle. Peter is able to walk on water but is overcome with fear and hesitation. He is "founding rock" and prime minister in Jesus' church but he is also called "Satan" and a "scandal" to Jesus (16:17-23). He is able to speak for Jesus but he also underestimates the necessity of reconciliation (18:21-22).

The encounter at Caesarea Philippi reveals that part of Peter's difficulty is accepting the cross of Jesus. In response to the first passion prediction Peter takes Jesus aside and

[34]Note that both Matthew and Luke (22:34) refer to only *one* cockcrow while Mark speaks of "two" (14:30). In the account of Peter's denial there is a report of only one cockcrow (Mark will call it the "second") and that may be the reason why Matthew and Luke speak of a single cockcrow in the prediction of Jesus (Matthew will follow through in his account of the denial; cf. below, 26:74). Some commentators suggest that Mark is more accurate in that he is referring to one of the Roman divisions of the nightwatch called "cockcrow"; the "second cockcrow" would be referring to the end of this third watch of the night.

[35]Cf. R. Brown, K. Donfried, J. Reumann, *Peter in the New Testament* (New York: Paulist, 1973), 75-107, and the discussion in D. Senior, *What Are They Saying about Matthew?*, 73-76.

attempts to silence him: "God forbid, Lord!" This shall never happen to you" (16:22). Matthew alone reports this statement of Peter. Jesus' equally vehement response demonstrates that we are not to take Peter's words as mere concern for his Master's safety but as a rejection of Jesus' stated notion of messiahship: "Get behind me, Satan! You are a scandal to me; for you are not on the side of God, but of humans" (16:23).

The connection between the Caesarea Philippi scene and Peter's statements in the passion are intriguing. In both instances Peter directly contradicts Jesus' own prophetic words. And while insisting on his determination to remain with Jesus, Peter uses words reminiscent of Jesus' own teaching on discipleship. Peter's words, "Even if I must die with you" (26:35) are not unlike Jesus' words, "If anyone would come after me, let him deny himself and take up his cross and follow me. For whoever would save his life will lose it, and whoever loses his life for my sake will find it..." (16:24-25; cf. similar sayings in 10:38-39). The passion will be a crisis for Peter. The first one to be called in the way of discipleship (4:18) will be the last one to leave Jesus. Peter's repeated insistence that he would never fail will be matched by vehement denials that he even knew Jesus (see below, 26:69-75).

III. Gethsemane: The Handing Over of the Son of Man (26:36-56)

The two events that take place in Gethsemane, the anguished prayer of Jesus (26:36-46) and his arrest (26:47-56), plunge the reader further into the mystery of the passion. With the prayer of Jesus preparation for the passion ends; the arrival of Judas and the mob begins the tortuous events of Jesus' suffering and eventual death.

> [36]Then Jesus went with them to a place called Gethsemane, and he said to his disciples, "Sit here, while I go yonder and pray." [37]And taking with him Peter and the two sons of Zebedee, he began to be sorrowful and

troubled. [38]Then he said to them, "My soul is very sorrowful, even to death; remain here, and watch with me." [39]And going a little farther he fell on his face and prayed, "My father, if it be possible, let this cup pass from me; nevertheless, not as I will, but as thou wilt." [40]And he came to the disciples and found them sleeping; and he said to Peter, "So, could you not watch with me one hour? [41]Watch and pray that you may not enter into temptation; the spirit indeed is willing, but the flesh is weak." [42]Again, for the second time, he went away and prayed, "My Father, if this cannot pass unless I drink it, thy will be done." [43]And again he came and found them sleeping, for their eyes were heavy. [44]So, leaving them again, he went away and prayed for the third time, saying the same words. [45]Then he came to the disciples and said to them, "Are you still sleeping and taking your rest? Behold, the hour is at hand, and the Son of Man is betrayed into the hands of sinners. [46]Rise, let us be going; see, my betrayer is at hand."

[47]While he was still speaking Judas came, one of the twelve, and with him a great crowd with swords and clubs, from the chief priests and the elders of the people [48]Now the betrayer had given them a sign, saying, "The one I shall kiss is the man; seize him." [49]And he came up to Jesus at once and said, "Hail, Master!" and he kissed him. [50]Jesus said to him, "Friend, why are you here?" Then they came up and laid hands on Jesus and seized him. [51]And behold, one of those who were with Jesus stretched out his hand and drew his sword, and struck the slave of the high priest and cut off his ear. [52]Then Jesus said to him, "Put your sword back into its place; for all who take the sword will perish by the sword. [53]Do you think that I cannot appeal to my Father, and he will at once send me more than twelve legions of angels? [54]But how then should the Scriptures be fulfilled, that it must be so?"[55]At that hour Jesus said to the crowds, "Have you come out as against a robber, with swords and clubs to capture me? Day after day I sat in the temple teaching, and you did not seize me. [56]But all this has taken place, that the Scriptures

of the prophets might be fulfilled." Then all the disciples forsook him and fled.

THE GETHSEMANE PRAYER (26:36-46)

Undoubtedly this is one of the most haunting events of the passion, indeed of the entire Gospel. The same Jesus who had majestically foretold his passion on the way to Jerusalem and repeated it the day before the passover festival (26:1-2), the one who at the supper just finished had declared he would drink wine in his Father's kingdom despite the separation of death (26:29), now in the darkness of Gethsemane crumples to the ground and prays that he will be delivered from that death.[36]

The spirit and drama of this passion prayer is the central focus of Matthew's presentation of the Gethsemane scene. His version is close to that of Mark but a number of significant alterations tend to edge the spotlight away from the numbing failure of the disciples (Mark's emphasis) toward the repeated and faithful prayer of Jesus.

This christological focus begins with the opening verse where Matthew highlights the initiative of Jesus as well as his bond with his disciples: "*Jesus* went *with them* to a place called Gethsemane..."). Matthew's wording of Jesus' instructions to his disciples — "Sit here, while I go yonder and pray" — may be a conscious allusion to the instruction Abraham gave to his followers when he arrived at the place for the sacrifice of his son Isaac (cf. Gn 22:5). The sacrifice of Isaac as a spectacular story of biblical faith was a favorite motif of later Jewish theology and Matthew may invoke it here as he prepares to demonstrate the extraordinary faith of God's Son.[37] In contrast to the story of Abraham and

---

[36]On the Gethsemane scene and its background, cf. the studies of R. Barbour, "Gethsemane in the Tradition of the Passion," *New Testament Studies* 16 (1969-70) 231-51; J. W. Holleron, *The Synoptic Gethsemane: A Critical Study* (Analecta Gregoriana; Rome: Gregorian University, 1973); D. Stanley, *Jesus in Gethsemane* (New York: Paulist, 1980).

[37]There is some dispute concerning the development of this tradition in the New Testament period and its possible influence on the evangelists. The "*Akedah Isaak*" ("The binding of Isaac") is a theological motif in the later Jewish targums of

Isaac, Jesus is both offerer and victim, an example of faith more brilliant than any biblical precedent.

An inner group of disciples accompanies Jesus deeper into the olive grove.[38] Peter and the two sons of Zebedee (26:37) were the first disciples Jesus had called (along with Andrew, Simon's brother; cf. 4:18-22 and their place in the list of the apostles, 10:2). The same trio had been privileged to be with Jesus on the mountaintop at the transfiguration (17:1-8). It is intriguing that these same disciples are singled out as having difficulty accepting Jesus' cross. Peter makes his protest to Jesus after the first passion prediction (16:22), and immediately after the third passion prediction the sons of Zebedee have their mother intercede to procure places of honor for them in Jesus' kingdom (20:20-28; note that in Mark's version James and John themselves pose the question to Jesus, cf. Mk 10:35). Their presence with Jesus in Gethsemane may imply that the disciples who witnessed Jesus' glory will now experience firsthand what it means to share Jesus' "cup," the only authentic means for entering into glory with him (the "cup" is mentioned in 20:22-23 and 26:27, 42).

The anguish of Jesus is forcefully described: "He began to be sorrowful and troubled" (26:37). His words to the disciples, "My soul is very sorrowful, even to death...", echo Psalm 42, one of the Old Testament's most eloquent prayers expressing the Psalmist's longing for God in the midst of suffering and fear of death:

> "My soul thirsts for God, for the living God. When shall I come and behold the face of God? My tears have been my food day and night, while people say to me continually,

Genesis 22. Isaac's willingness to be sacrificed and the exemplary faith of Abraham were seen to have atoning power for Israel. On this tradition, see the discussion in R. Le Deaut, *La Nuit Pascale, Essai sur la signification de la Pâque juive a partir du Targum d'Exode XII, 42* (Analecta Biblica 22 Rome: Biblical Institute Press, 1963).

[38] Matthew and Mark refer only to "Gethsemane"; Luke speaks of the "Mount of Olives" (22:39), while John refers to a "garden" (18:1). The name "Gethsemane" means "oil press," probably indicating a grove or "garden" of olive trees on the western slope of the Mount of Olives.

'Where is your God?'...Why are you sorrowful, my soul, and why are you disquieted within me? Hope in God; for I shall again praise him, my help and my God...."

The ominous phrase "even unto death" is not found in the original and represents a Christian adaptation of the psalm as it was read in the light of Jesus' prayer before his death.[39] Following Mark's lead, Matthew does not hesitate to present Jesus praying a prayer of lament, one of the boldest forms of Jewish piety.[40] As generations of faithful Jews had done before him, Jesus prays in the midst of crisis, honestly expressing his fear and bafflement before the darkness of death.

The three disciples are asked to "remain here, and watch *with me*" (26:38; the latter phrase is not found in Mark's parallel, cf. 14:34). The emphasis Matthew has placed on the bond between Jesus and his disciples throughout the opening scenes of the passion narrative continues here.[41] The command to "watch" or, literally, "stay awake" recalls the urgent instructions of Jesus' final discourse. There the disciples were told to be as alert householders and to "Watch-...for you do not know on what day your Lord is coming" (24:42-43). The parable of the wise and foolish maidens closes with the same type of exhortation: "Watch therefore, for you know neither the day nor the hour" (25:13) This connection between the final discourse and the passion reflects the evangelist's conviction that the death and resurrection of Jesus are the decisive events of sacred history.[42] In

[39] Early Christian writers freely adapted the Old Testament to fit the circumstances of Jesus' life and their own experience, and Matthew is no exception. On Matthew's use of the Old Testament, cf. the discussion in D. Senior, *What Are They Saying about Matthew?*, 37-46.

[40] On the lament psalms in the passion narrative, cf. D. Senior, *The Passion of Jesus in the Gospel of Mark*, 70-73; on the background of the laments and their theology, cf. C. Stuhlmueller, *Psalms*, Vol. 1 (Old Testament Message 21; Wilmington: Michael Glazier, 1983), 35-39 and J. P. Miller, "Trouble and Woe: Interpreting Biblical Laments," *Interpretation* 37 (1983), 32-45.

[41] Cf. 26:18 ("with my disciples"), 26:20 ("with the twelve disciples"), 26:29 ("with you").

[42] Cf. above, Part I, pp. 38-40; Part III, pp. 181-84.

a real sense the endtime for which the community is to watch is now to appear, as the moment of Jesus' arrest looms. This is the *kairos,* the opportune time which Jesus awaited (26:18), that moment in which Jesus' decisive and faithful act of love would lead the world to final salvation.

Jesus now begins to pray, doing himself what he had taught others to do.[43] Moving some distance from the three disciples he "fell on his face" (26:39; contrast Mark's "he fell on the ground," 14:35), a phrase used in the Bible to connote intense adoration and respect (see, for example, Gn 17:3, 17; Nm 14:5; 2 Sm 9:6; I Kgs 18:39. Jesus prays: "My Father, if it be possible, let this cup pass from me; nevertheless, not as I will, but as thou wilt."

The spirit and content of this first prayer of Jesus are drawn from the parallel found in Mark (14:36) but Matthew shapes it to fit the mode of his own Gospel. Jesus addresses God as "My Father," a translation of the intimate Aramaic word, *Abba,* used by Mark.[44] Twice before in Matthew's Gospel Jesus had directly addressed God as his "Father" in prayer. The first is found in the Sermon on the Mount where Jesus teaches the disciples to pray in the model of the Lord's Prayer (6:9-13). The spirit and form of this fundamental prayer certainly influence Matthew's rendition of the Gethsemane prayer. Both prayers are prayers of obedience ("your kingdom come," "your will be done") as well as prayers for deliverance from the final "test" and from "evil."[45] The "Father" is addressed again in 11:25, a prayer of thanksgiving for the revelation withheld from the "wise and understanding" but lavished on Jesus.

Reference to God as "Father" is a hallmark of Matthew's

---

[43]Insistence on doing what one teaches is a strong motif of Matthew's Gospel. Jesus explicitly commands this in 5:19 and condemns the hypocrisy of the scribes and Pharisees who "preach, but do not practice" (23:3). On this cf. above, Part I, pp. 35-36. In 21:22, Jesus had taught the disciples: "And whatever you ask in prayer, you will receive, if you have faith."

[44]On this unique word as an address in prayer and its implications, see the literature quoted in D. Senior, *The Passion in the Gospel of Mark,* 73-75.

[45]On the Lord's prayer in Matthew, cf. J. Jeremias, *The Prayers of Jesus* (Philadelphia: Fortress, 1978), 82-107; P. Harner, *Understanding the Lord's Prayer* (Phiadelphia: Fortress, 1975).

Gospel (the title is used some 53 times in Matthew compared to only 6 in Mark).[46] It matches the Gospel's equally strong emphasis on Jesus' identity as "Son of God." As we shall note, Matthew's stress on the Father-Son metaphor serves Matthew's protrayal of Jesus as the obedient Israelite who faithfully pursues God's justice, even to death.[47] That is certainly the mood in Gethsemane; even as Jesus wrestles with the specter of impending death and prays for deliverance, he addresses God as a faithful Son.

The thrust of Jesus' prayer is that God would remove "the cup." The "cup" clearly refers to Jesus' suffering and death (cf. 20:22-23; 26:27-28). The Gospel does not state that the source of Jesus' anguish was the specter of humanity's future sins, as is sometimes suggested in commentaries on this text. Something much more baffling and provocative is asserted here: Jesus, faithful son of God, is also a child of humanity and therefore he fears the death that threatens his mortal existence. The Gethsemane prayer is a strong antidote to any portrayal of Jesus that dilutes his humanness.

At the same moment Jesus anxiously prays to be delivered from death he also prays that God's will be done. A mixture of faith and frailty has always characterized authentic Christian piety. The phrases "if it be possible" and "nevertheless, not as I will, but as thou wilt" strongly affirm the obedience that has animated the Matthean Jesus from the opening scenes of the Gospel.[48] Jesus had taught the disciples that the one "who does the will of my Father who is in heaven" and not those who simply mouth pious words would be the ones to enter the kingdom (7:21). "Whoever does the will of my Father in heaven" belonged to the family of Jesus because that was the spirit of his whole existence

---

[46]Cf. further, J. Jeremias, *The Prayers of Jesus*, 11-65; D. Senior, *The Passion Narrative according to Matthew*, 107-108. On the issue of Jesus' use of male imagery for God, cf. R. Hammerton-Kelly, *God the Father: Theology and Patriarchy in the Teaching of Jesus* (Overtures to Biblical Theology; Philadelphia: Fortress, 1979).

[47]Cf. below, pp. 164-66.

[48]On obedience as a motif of Matthew's presentation of Jesus, cf. above, Part I, pp. 26-30.

(13:50). Jesus had come "not to destroy but to fulfill" the Scriptures (5:17), searching them for the will of God and faithfully bringing that will to expression in action. Even as Jesus clutches the earth in sorrow and anguish, that deep abiding spirit of fidelity is not extinguished.

The first prayer completed, Jesus returns to the three disciples and finds them "sleeping" (26:40). His words to Peter make it clear that not just physical sleep is the issue here: "So, could you not watch with me one hour? Watch and pray that you may not enter into temptation; the spirit indeed is willing, but the flesh is weak." Instead of being alert in prayer and preparing for the coming of the *kairos*, the disciples are overcome with sleep and will eventually be swept away (see Jesus' warning in 24:36-44). The cause of this is not an unwilling "spirit" but the weakness of "flesh." This polarity between "spirit" and "flesh" as a way of expressing the struggle between good and evil in the human heart is typical of Jewish texts in the intertestamental period. Unlike the classical division of "soul" and "body," the polarities of "flesh" and "spirit" represent not separable component parts of a human being but two opposing tendencies struggling for domination within the one body-person.

This view of the disciples as caught in the tension of "flesh" and "spirit" is very compatible with the way Matthew portrays the disciples throughout his Gospel. The evangelist's special term for the disciples is "little faith." They are neither "unbelieving" (as Mark will sometime describe them) nor fully believing. "Fear" and "hesitation" can crimp the faith of the disciples, as it seems to now in the face of the passion.[49]

Jesus asks them to pray "that they may not enter into temptation," a phrase that echoes the sixth petition of the Lord's prayer (6:13). In both instances the word translated here as "temptation" is the Greek word *peirasmos,* meaning

---

[49]A good example of this is Mt 14:28-31 where Peter displays both faults as he senses the power of the storm. On the theme of "little faith" and Matthew's portrayal of the disciples, cf. above, Part I, pp. 44-45.

"test." In the Lord's prayer, as here, "temptation" or "test" does not refer merely to the passing seductions of evil but to that ultimate test, the crisis of the final days when the true strength and commitment of the community will be determined. Since the chaos and trials of history may be enough to engulf the believer (see, for example of Mt. 24:9-13, 15-24, esp. 24:22, 24), they must pray that God deliver them from such overwhelming evil. There is a sober assessment of evil here drawn not only from the apocalyptic symbolism of Jesus' words but undoubtedly reflecting the turbulent experience of Matthew's community.

Jesus leaves the disciples and returns to pray a "second time" (26:42). At this point in the scene Matthew's special interest becomes clear in contrast to Mark's account. Mark seems to focus on Jesus' repeated discovery of the sleeping disciples; the second prayer of Jesus is not recorded (Mark simply states that Jesus prays, "saying the same words"; Mk 14:39) while his return to the disciples is enumerated ("the third time," Mk. 14:40). Matthew, by contrast, concentrates on the content and the repetition of Jesus' faithful prayer rather than on his return to the sleeping disciples.

The content of the second prayer is similar to the first.[50] However, there is a progression: the words "if it can*not* pass unless I drink it" show the mounting resignation of Jesus before the inevitability of his death (compare 26:38, "if it is possible, let this cup pass"). The spirit of the Lord's Prayer also moves strongly through this second prayer; the words "thy will be done" are identical to the third petition of the Lord's Prayer (6:10). Matthew continues to present Jesus as the living example of the prayer he had taught his disciples.

The scene moves rapidly to its conclusion. Jesus returns again to find the disciples still sleeping (26:43). Matthew's explanation "for their eyes were heavy" is more tolerant

---

[50] In fact, Matthew seems to fashion the contents of the prayer from the indirect discourse Mark provides in his report of the first prayer; cf. Mk 14:35, where Jesus prays "that, if it were possible, the hour might pass from him." On Matthew's use of Mark in this scene, cf. D. Senior, *The Passion Narrative according to Matthew*, 100-19.

than Mark's phrase: "and they did not know what to answer him" (Mk 14:40).[51] Yet again Jesus returns to prayer, "a third time...saying the same words." Matthew constructs this verse from material provided by Mark ("the third time"; cf. Mk 14:41; "saying the same words"; cf. Mk. 14:39) but shifts it around so that the focus remains on Jesus' repeated prayer.

His threefold prayer complete, Jesus returns to the disciples and rouses them for the moment of the *"kairos"* that will now explode upon the olive grove (26:45). Once again Matthew portrays Jesus with majestic determination in the face of threat and death: "Behold the hour is at hand, and the Son of Man is betrayed into the hands of sinners. Rise, let us be going; see, my betrayer is at hand" (26:45-46). His faithful prayer has made him "awake" and "watchful" as the decisive hour approaches.[52] Jesus' words identify the hour with Judas' arrival: the verses are in close parallel, "Behold, the hour is at hand" — "Behold my betrayer is at hand" (the same Greek word *idou*, "behold" prefaces each statement). Throughout the Gospel it has been the arrest, the moment of the "handing over," that has been the focus of Jesus' prophetic predictions. This was the fateful moment when Jesus and the forces of death would meet; at this moment Jesus would lose his freedom and begin the fateful, swift journey towards his death. The night of the arrest was indeed the moment when the decisive *kairos* of Jesus had come.[53] The subsequent scene would be a vivid demonstration of how different would be the responses of Jesus and his disciples.

---

[51] This explanation is the same as that used in Mark's transfiguration account as a comment on Peter's confused response to the vision (see Mk 9:6). Throughout his Gospel Mark, in contrast to Matthew, stresses the incomprehension of the disciples.

[52] Note that the term "hour" in this context has the same eschatological connotation as the word *"kairos"* ("time"); cf. above, pp. 60-61.

[53] Matthew's wording is exactly parallel in these three key texts:
"My *kairos* is approaching" (26:18)
"The hour is approaching" (26:45)
"My betrayer is approaching" (26:46).

THE ARREST (26:47-56)

At the very moment Jesus is rousing his disciples from sleep and warning them of the arrival of the fateful hour, Judas and the armed mob enter Gethsemane (26:47). As has been the case throughout Matthew's passion narrative, the evangelist highlights the prophetic knowledge and majestic power of Jesus even when he seems to be the victim of his foes. This will be especially true in this important scene, the actual beginning of Jesus' *kairos*. At the very moment he is arrested, Jesus declares his absolute freedom to carry out his messianic mission in accordance with God's will.

The tragedy of Judas' betrayal is pressed upon the reader again: he is "one of the twelve" yet he is associated with an armed mob "from the chief priests and the elders of the people," the ones who had engineered the final plot against Jesus' life (see 26:3-5). Even more tragic is that Judas uses a sign of friendship as the signal for treachery. He instructs the armed mob, "The one I shall kiss is the man; seize him" (26:48).

Matthew continues to show his special interest in Judas. As in Mark's account the betrayer boldly comes up to Jesus and kisses him. But Matthew adds to the exchange between Jesus and his lost disciple. Judas twists a greeting of friendship, "Hail, Rabbi!" into a death sign (26:49). The reader can only recall the question Judas had put to Jesus at the supper, "It isn't I, is it, Rabbi?" (26:25) and remember the negative significance of using the term "Rabbi" in Matthew's Gospel.[54]

The wording of Jesus' reply (26:50, found only in Matthew) is somewhat obscure in the Greek.[55] Perhaps the best

---

[54]The term is never used as a positive title in Matthew; cf. above, pp. 63-64.

[55]It is uncertain whether the words of Jesus are to be taken as a statement or a question, and the words themselves, involving the unusual combination of a preposition, relative pronoun, and finite verb are difficult to translate. The translation suggested here takes the words to be a declarative sentence and presumes that there is an ellipse in the sentence which must be supplied by the reader. The "ellipse" is the very action of Judas (the kiss of betrayal) to which Jesus refers: literally, "for [this, i.e., the kiss of betrayal] you are here." For a detailed discussion, cf. D. Senior, *The Passion Narrative according to Matthew*, 125-27.

translation would be: "Friend, this [i.e., the treacherous kiss Judas has just given Jesus] is what you are here for." Jesus addresses Judas as "friend" even as the disciple betrays Jesus and crudely violates the bond of love and reverence between master and disciple. At the same time, Jesus displays that penetrating knowledge of the passion events so evident in Matthew's story. By having Jesus respond to Judas, the evangelist has, in effect, delayed the onrush of the crowd until after Jesus has spoken (contrast Mk 14:46 where they lay hands on Jesus as soon as Judas kisses Jesus); only "then" are they free to come up to Jesus and arrest him (26:50). Even though the enemies of Jesus appear to have him as their victim they have no real power over him.[56]

The importance of this scene for Matthew's theology is seen in the events that follow immediately upon the arrest. The evangelist significantly expands the strange incident of the sword reported by Mark (see Mk 14:47). In Mark's version the use of the sword seems to be an accident. One of "those who stood by" draws a sword and cuts off the ear of the high priest's servant. Mark seems to refer *not* to a disciple of Jesus but to a "bystander" *with the mob* as the one who drew the sword. The phrase "those who stood by" is not a designation for the disciples in Mark and he has already identified the mob as the ones bearing "swords and clubs" (see Mk 14:43, 48). Thus for Mark the incident is part of the mayhem of the crowd scene; this chaos and violence prompt Jesus to reproach his captors for coming out "as against a robber, with swords and clubs to capture me" (Mk 14:48).[57]

This reproach of Jesus to the crowd and the clear distinction between his own comportment and the violence of his captors provide Matthew with an opportunity for introducing some important teaching. The incident is introduced with a dramatic flourish ("And behold.." 26:51); it is no

---

[56]This presentation is similar to John's account where Jesus takes full initiative at the moment of arrest, giving permission for his captors to arrest him and demanding that his disciples be allowed to leave freely: cf. John 18:2-12.

[57]Cf. D. Senior, *The Passion of Jesus in the Gospel of Mark*, 82-83.

longer simply a member of the armed mob who draws the sword but "one of those who were with Jesus." The violence of the crowd has infested Jesus' own disciples and one of them, in a feeble attempt to protect his master, lashes out at Jesus' enemies.[58]

That use of violence by a disciple provokes Jesus' words found only in Matthew's Gospel (26:52-54):

> "Put your sword back into its place; for all who take the sword will perish by the sword. Do you think that I cannot appeal to my Father, and he will at once send me more than twelve legions of angels? But how then should the Scriptures be fulfilled, that it must be so?"

This important teaching moment demonstrates the absolute consistency and integrity of the Matthean Jesus: as he teaches so he acts (an emphasis of this Gospel: cf. 5:19 and, negatively, 23:3). The use of violence to further Jesus' mission, even to protect his life, is clearly rejected. The sword is to be put back into its place "for all who take the sword will perish by the sword." The saying has a proverbial ring to it and some have noted its similarity to Apocalypse 13:10, "If anyone is to be taken captive, to captivity he goes; if any slays with the sword, with the sword must he be slain."

But a more immediate inspiration for these words of Jesus can be found earlier in Matthew's own Gospel. In the Sermon on the Mount Jesus had clearly declared that the use of violence was not to be the way of those committed to God's rule. Jesus had come to "fulfill" the law and the prophets (5:17), that is, to offer a new and definitive interpretation of what God asked of his people. Illustrations of this new "holiness" (literally "justice," cf. 5:20) are given in the series of antitheses in which Jesus' new interpretation of the law is contrasted with previous interpretations. Where

---

[58]We have already noted that Matthew has emphasized the bonds between Jesus and his disciples precisely by repeated use of phrases such as "with him" or "with me" or "with you"(cf. above, p. 61). The identification of the sword bearer as a disciple is also made by Luke (22:49) and John (18;10); the latter identifies him as Peter!

the law of talion ("an eye for an eye and a tooth for a tooth") had attempted to regulate retaliation for injury, making the retribution in proportion to the injury, Jesus' new teaching rejected such violent retribution altogether: "But I say to you, do not resist one who is evil.. But if any one strikes you on the right cheek, turn to him the other also..." (5:39). And in a text of capital importance in Matthew's theology, Jesus proclaimed, "But I say to you, love your enemies and pray for those who persecute you, so that you may be sons [and daughters] of your Father who is in heaven for he makes his sun rise on the evil and on the good, and sends rain on the just and on the unjust" (5:43-45).[59]

In the Sermon on the Mount and in Gethsemane Jesus explicitly rejects the option of violence. Rather than continue the endless chain of retribution, with violence spawning yet more violence ("those who live by the sword, die by the sword"), Jesus prophetically breaks the chain. His power is not that of the sword. If it were he would not have to depend on the feeble swordplay of his twelve apostles but could appeal to his Father and have at hand "twelve legions of angels" (26:53).

But to choose violence would not be Jesus' option. If he had, "how then should the Scriptures be fulfilled, that it must be so?" (26:54). In the Sermon on the Mount Jesus had already declared that the "fulfilled" law and the prophets pointed toward a world in which violence and retribution had no place. The world in which God ruled would not be dominated by alienation. And in that same olive grove Jesus had bound himself to his Father's will; he would not choose the ordinary human way, the way of violence, but God's way, the way of the Father who lavishes his gracious compassion and forgiveness on good and bad alike, just as the sun and the rain drench all of creation (5:45).

Thus Matthew uses the moment of the arrest to reflect on Jesus' own response to violence. Here in his final act as a free man Jesus validates his own teaching not only in word but in action. His refusal to use the sword was not a "passive"

[59]On this profound text of Matthew, cf. above, Part I, p. 29.

gesture but a fully active one. He does not accept the terms and values of his enemies. He calls his betrayer a "friend" (26:50) and challenges the violence of his captors: "Have you come out as against a robber, with swords and clubs to capture me? Day after day I sat in the temple teaching, and you did not seize me" (26:55). "Sitting" (contrast Mk 14:49) was a position of authority for a Jewish teacher.[60] Throughout chapters 21-23 Matthew had presented Jesus in sharp and open conflict with his opponents as he taught in the temple area. Jesus' "weapons" were not those of physical violence but the power of truth and compassion. Because they feared that kind of power and its attractiveness to the people, Jesus' opponents had not dared to arrest him in the open (see 21:45-46; 26:5).

The arrest scene closes with a word of Jesus and an action by the disciples. In Matthew's version Jesus declares: "But all this has taken place that the Scriptures of the prophets might be fulfilled" (26:56; contrast Mk 14:49, "But let the Scriptures be fulfilled."). Emphasis falls on the sweep of Jesus' words: "*all*" of this has happened to fulfill the Scriptures. The moment of the arrest condenses the entire passion of Jesus. At this chilling moment Jesus is handed over to the power of death. Yet "all of this" — the entire event of his sufferings and death — is not arbitrary violence nor absurd tragedy but mysteriously fulfills the "Scriptures of the prophets."

This unique designation for the Scriptures fits into Matthew's perspective. All of the explicit "fulfillment quotations" in Matthew's Gospel are drawn from the writings of the prophets.[61] And for Matthew the entire Old Testament

[60]See, for example, Mt 5:1; 13:1-2; 23:2 (referring to the scribes and Pharisees who "sit on Moses seat" and are, therefore, worthy of respect).

[61]Of the Old Testament citations introduced with Matthew's fulfillment formula, cf. 1:22 (Is 7:14), 2:6 (Mi 5:2), 2:15 (Hos 11:1), 2:17 (Jer 31:15), 2:23 (it is difficult to assign any single Old Testament text to this example; some authors suggest Matthew was alluding to the "sprig" referred to in Is 11:1, playing on the similarity between "Nazarene" and the Hebrew word for "sprig," *neser*), 4:15-16 (Is 9:1-2), 8:17 (Is 53:4), 12:18-21 (Is 42:1-4), 13:35 (Ps 78:2, a psalm attributed to Asaph the seer [cf. 2 Chr 29:30]), 21:5 (Is 62:11; Zec 9:9), 27:9-10 (Zec 11:12-13; on this text, cf. our discussion below). On Matthew's use of the Old Testament, cf. D. Senior, *What Are They Saying about Matthew?*, 37-46, and above, Part I.

has a prophetic aura because Jesus was the fulfillment of its promises. All of the sacred history of Israel was compressed into Jesus, God's Son, and found its authentic fulfillment in him. Therefore Matthew's Jesus could declare: "I have not come to destroy the law and the prophets but to fulfill them" (5:17).[62] Because the passion of Jesus was the final expression of Jesus' mission of salvation the evangelist presents it as the ultimate fulfillment of the "Scriptures of the prophets."

The scene ends with a terse statement that jerks the reader away from the majesty of Jesus' declaration and back into the brutal reality of the passion: "Then all the disciples forsook him and fled" (26:56). By placing the flight of the disciples after Jesus' words and by introducing it with the link word "then," Matthew seems to imply that only after Jesus had spoken are these events free to happen (as at the moment of arrest, cf. above 26:50). Once again the Gospel implies that underneath the chaos and failure of the scene pulsates God's mysterious providence.

IV. Trial before the Sanhedrin (26:57—27:10)

The course of action in the passion drama now moves from the slope of the Mount of Olives back to the city of Jerusalem, to the house of Caiaphas the High Priest. Here the conflict between Jesus and his opponents will come to its most bitter expression. But Matthew's focus is not simply on the opponents of Jesus. The center of attention remains on Jesus who fearlessly confesses his identity as Messiah, Son of God, and triumphant Son of Man while his opponents, Peter, and finally Judas provide tragic counterpoints to Jesus' integrity. Three of the scenes take place in a single location: the interrogation and mockery before the Sanhedrin (26:57-68); the denial of Peter (26:69-75); and the final verdict of the Sanhedrin and the handing over of Jesus to Pilate (27:1-2). The fate of Judas (27:3-10) is a tragic inter-

---

[62]On the importance of this text in Matthew, cf. above, Part I, pp. 26-27.

lude that bridges the transfer of Jesus from the house of Caiaphas to the trial before Pilate.

⁵⁷Then those who had seized Jesus led him to Caiaphas the High Priest, where the scribes and the elders had gathered. ⁵⁸But Peter followed him at a distance, as far as the courtyard of the High Priest, and going inside he sat with the guards to see the end. ⁵⁹Now the chief priests and the whole council sought false testimony against Jesus that they might put him to death, ⁶⁰but they found none, though many false witnesses came forward. At last two came forward ⁶¹and said, "This fellow said, 'I am able to destroy the temple of God, and to rebuild it in three days.'" ⁶²And the High Priest stood up and said, "Have you no answer to make? What is it that these men testify against you?" ⁶³But Jesus was silent. And the High Priest said to him, "I adjure you by the living God, tell us if you are the Christ, the Son of God." ⁶⁴Jesus said to him, "You have said so. But I tell you, hereafter you will see the Son of Man seated at the right hand of Power, and coming on the clouds of heaven." ⁶⁵Then the High Priest tore his robes, and said, "He has uttered blasphemy. Why do we still need witnesses? You have now heard his blasphemy. ⁶⁶What is your judgment?" They answered, "He deserves death." ⁶⁷Then they spat in his face, and struck him; and some slapped him, ⁶⁸saying, "Prophesy to us, you Christ! Who is it that struck you?"

⁶⁹Now Peter was sitting outside in the courtyard. And a maid came up to him, and said, "You also were with Jesus the Galilean." ⁷⁰But he denied it before them all, saying, "I do not know what you mean." ⁷¹And when he went out to the porch, another maid saw him, and she said to the bystanders, "This man was with Jesus of Nazareth." ⁷²And again he denied it with an oath, "I do not know the man." ⁷³After a little while the bystanders came up and said to Peter, "Certainly you are also one of them, for your accent betrays you." ⁷⁴Then he began to invoke a curse on himself and to swear, "I do not know the man."

And immediately the cock crowed. [75]And Peter remembered the saying of Jesus, "Before the cock crows, you will deny me three times." And he went out and wept bitterly.

(27:1) When morning came, all the chief priests and the elders of the people took counsel against Jesus to put him to death; [2]and they bound him and led him away and delivered him to Pilate the governor.

[3]When Judas, his betrayer, saw that he was condemned, he repented and brought back the thirty pieces of silver to the chief priests and the elders [4]saying, "I have sinned in betraying innocent blood." They said, "What is that to us? See to it yourself." [5]And throwing down the pieces of silver in the temple, he departed; and he went and hanged himself. [6]But the chief priests, taking the pieces of silver, said, "It is not lawful to put them into the treasury, since they are blood money." [7]So they took counsel, and bought with them the potter's field, to bury strangers in. [8]Therefore that field has been called the Field of Blood to this day. [9]Then was fulfilled what had been spoken by the prophet Jeremiah, saying, "And they took the thirty pieces of silver, the price of him on whom a price had been set by some of the sons of Israel, [10]and they gave them for the potter's field, as the Lord directed me."

Interrogation by the Sanhedrin (26:57-68).

The exact nature of the session Matthew now relates is difficult to determine. There is reason to suspect that historically this was not a full-blown trial but a strategy session in which the Jewish leaders questioned Jesus and deliberated on what course of action to take against him. [63] In any event Matthew draws his version of the "trial" from his source Mark, introducing, as he consistently does, a number of stylistic changes and some that turn the story more in the direction of his perspective.

[63] On the historical issues surrounding the trial, cf. D. Senior, *The Passion of Jesus in the Gospel of Mark*, 88-90.

The armed crowd who had come with Judas to Gethsemane now take him to the house of Caiaphas the High Priest.[64] Here the members of the ruling assembly, the Sanhedrin, were gathered.[65] Matthew prepares for the wrenching contrasts of this section by immediately referring to Peter's hesitant presence. The leader of the apostles who had pledged, "Even if I must die with you, I will not deny you" (26:35), still follows Jesus but "at a distance" (26:58). He goes into the courtyard of the High Priest's residence and sits with the guards "to see the end." Mark had provided the colorful detail of Peter "warming himself at the fire" (Mk 14:54). Matthew, as he frequently does, eliminates such homespun information in preference for an explicit statement of Peter's intention. His bold entry into the circle of Jesus' captors will be in direct contrast to his remorseful departure (26:75).

Matthew does not mince words about the intent of the Sanhedrin: the purpose of the meeting is to seek "false testimony" against Jesus in order to put him to death (26:59; contrast Mk 14:55 where this is put much less directly). Matthew's consistently negative portrayal of the Jewish leaders continues.[66] Even though a number of false witnesses come forward their testimony is apparently too ineffective to be used against Jesus.

Finally, though, two witnesses come forward and make a dramatic claim against Jesus (26:60-61). It is significant that Matthew does not label these witnesses as false (contrast Mark 14:57-58). There are "two" of them because according to Jewish law two witnesses were needed for condemnation in capital cases (cf. Dt 17:16). They accuse Jesus of making the claim, "I am able to destroy the temple of God and to

[64] As mentioned above (cf. 26:3) Matthew and John are the only evangelists to explicitly mention the name of Caiaphas.

[65] The Roman procurator had ultimate political power over the province of Judea (where Jerusalem was located) but the Sanhedrin apparently had extensive jurisdiction over religious and other aspects of Jewish life. The extent of the Sanhedrin's jurisdiction in the first century, particularly in the case of capital punishment, is much debated.

[66] Cf. Part I, ; this negative portrayal has obvious implications for contemporary interpretation of the Gospel; on this cf. below, pp. 177-81.

rebuild it in three days" (26:61). The accusation is carefully worded; the claim is not that I *will* destroy the temple but that *I am able to* (contrast Mk 14:58). Nor is there any distinction between a temple "made with hands" and one "not made with hands" (as in Mk 14:58). In Matthew's version, Jesus' alleged statement is that he has the *power* to destroy the Jerusalem temple.

Nowhere in the Gospel of Matthew does Jesus, in fact, make a statement exactly like this; it is probable that Matthew (similar to Mark) envisages the testimony of the two witnesses as false in intent. However, Matthew's formulation of the accusation allows its ironic truth to be very apparent to the reader. Matthew had presented Jesus as entering triumphantly into the Jerusalem temple to the acclaim of the crowds, purifying it of corruption and opening its doors to "the blind and the lame" (a potent reform mentioned only in Matthew, cf. 21:14). Jesus ominously accused the leaders of making God's house "a den of thieves," words taken from Jer 7:11 where the prophet had warned the temple leaders that Yahweh could destroy the sanctuary in Jerusalem just as he had done at Shiloh. And there is little doubt in the Gospel that Jesus' messianic authority extends to the temple itself (something the leaders ineffectively challenge; cf. the debate about authority in 21:23-27). He is the "Son of Man" who is "Lord of the Sabbath" (12:8); he is the one David the king called "Lord" (22:41-46). The entire discourse on judgment and the future of the world (chapters 24-25) began with Jesus' prophetic words warning that the buildings of the temple: ". . . will not be left here one stone upon another, that will not be thrown down" (24:2).

There is evidence that some Jewish traditions envisaged a purifying destruction and rebuilding of the temple in the messianic age.[67] The significance of this accusation against

---

[67] Cf. further, L. Gaston, *No Stone upon Another. Studies in the Significance of the Fall of Jerusalem in the Synoptic Gospels* (Supplements to Novum Testamentum 23; Leiden: Brill, 1970), 147-54; D. Juel, *Messiah and Temple. The Trial of Jesus in the Gospel of Mark* (SBL Dissertation Series 31; Missoula: Scholars Press, 1977), 169-209.

Jesus in his trial may rest on this motif; Jesus' alleged threats against the temple were coupled to his messianic claims. Matthew uses the temple accusation (already found in Mark) as a way of asserting Jesus' messianic power: he *is able* to destroy the temple.

But the fact that Matthew writes his Gospel after the Roman siege of Jerusalem and the ensuing destruction of the Temple in A.D. 70 adds another layer of irony to this point in the trial. The evangelist apparently interprets this tragedy as punishment on Israel for its rejection of Jesus. In Matthew's version of some of Jesus' parables this vantage point seems to emerge: the "owner of the vineyard" not only takes away the vineyard from the tenants who reject his messengers and kill his son, but he comes and puts "those wretches to a miserable death" (Mt 21:41; contrast Mk 12:9; Lk 20:16). In the parable of the wedding feast, the king grows angry at those first invited who not only turn down the invitation but brutalize and kill the king's messengers (22:6). To punish them the king dispatches his troops "and destroyed those murderers and burned their city" (Mt 22:7; not found in Luke's version of the story, 14:15-24). As we shall discuss below, Matthew even presents the people themselves as accepting responsibility for Jesus' death (see 27:24-25). For Matthew, therefore, the fate of the temple is directly linked to the death of Jesus. The destruction of the temple will be an event signalling the final age (cf. below 27:51-53). A new temple can be built in three days, just as the death of Jesus will be transformed into resurrection triumph. But the demise of the temple is also an event whereby the sin of rejecting the good news of salvation reaps its punishment. [68]

The testimony of the two witnesses triggers the intervention of the High Priest (26:62). He challenges Jesus, demanding some response to the allegations. But Jesus continues to remain silent; it may be that the Gospel wishes

---

[68] It should be obvious that Matthew's theology has some dangerous side effects, especially its potential for being interpreted in an anti-semitic fashion. On this point, cf. our discussion below, Part III, pp. 177-81.

to remind the reader of the Suffering Servant who stood silent before his captors (cf. Is 53:7).

That eloquent silence pushes Caiaphas to the decisive question: "I adjure you by the living God, tell us if you are the Christ, the Son of God" (26:23). Matthew has significantly reshaped the High Priest's question (compare Mk 14:61, "Are you the Christ, Son of the Blessed?"). In Matthew's version the High Priest takes an oath. In the Sermon on the Mount Jesus had taught his disciples, "Do not swear at all, either by heaven, for it is the throne of God, or by the earth, for it is his footstool, or by Jerusalem, for it is the city of the Great King." For the one who lives by the truth a simple "yes" or "no" suffices (6:33-37). That lesson seemed to be lost on the scribes and Pharisees whom Jesus castigated for their elaborate system of oaths (23:16-22). Now the High Priest falls into the same manner of speech (as will Peter in the next scene).

The terms of his question are equally significant: he demands to know if Jesus is "the Christ, the Son of God."[69] These two major titles for Jesus were grouped once before in the Gospel when Peter made his solemn confession at Caesarea Philippi (16:16). The term "Christ" refers, of course, to Jesus' identity as the promised Messiah or royal liberator of Israel. Matthew has clearly identified Jesus as the fulfillment of this promise from the very beginning of his Gospel. The opening verse trumpets the "origin of Jesus *Christ*" (1:1). The entire infancy narrative revolves around Jesus' messianic identity, as the magi come to do the newly born king homage and Herod attempts to destroy this supposed claimant to his throne.[70] Later in the Gospel Jesus' ministry is summarized as "the works of the Christ" (11:2) when the imprisoned John hears of Jesus' mission and sends disciples

---

[69] On Matthew's use of these titles, cf. J. Kingsbury, *Matthew: Structure, Christology, Kingdom*, 40-127, and his later restatement in *Jesus Christ in Matthew, Mark, and Luke* (Proclamation Commentaries; Philadelphia: Fortress, 1981), 61-93. On the whole issue of Christology in Matthew, cf. the range of views presented in D. Senior, *What Are They Saying about Matthew?*, 56-66.

[70] Cf. explicit references in 1:16, 17, 18; 2:4; on the infancy narrative and its connection to the passion cf. above, Part I, pp. 18-23.

to ask if he is the one "who is to come." When Peter acclaims Jesus as the Messiah, Jesus accepts that designation (16:20), even while beginning to teach the disciples about the passion. And beyond such explicit uses of the title, it is obvious on every page of the Gospel that Matthew views Jesus as the Messiah who fulfills Israel's hopes for salvation and ushers in the final age of history.

The "Son of God" title is also an important designation for Jesus in Matthew. On two occasions the demons address Jesus in this fashion. In the desert, Satan prefaces his tests with the challenge "If you are the Son of God..." (4:3, 6); a formulation that will be used by Jesus' mockers on Golgotha; see below, 27:40). And when Jesus approaches, the Gadarene demoniacs recoil in fear and cry out, "What have you to do with us, O Son of God? Have you come here to torment us before the time?" (8:29). The title is also found on the lips of the disciples. As Jesus walks across the chaotic sea and rescues Peter from being engulfed because of his fear, the disciples acclaim in worship: "Truly you are the Son of God." This powerful confession of Jesus echoes that of the centurion and his companions at the moment of Jesus' death (see below, 27:54).

One might add to these instances of the title the several references to Jesus as "son" where the designation "of God" is assumed but not stated, as for example when the "voice from heaven" acclaims Jesus at the moment of his baptism (3:17) and transfiguration (17:5). The bond between God and Jesus in the metaphorical language of "father" and "son" is particularly important for Matthew's theology. This is most clearly expressed in chapter 11 where Jesus breaks out in a prayer of gratitude to his "Father" for having revealed "hidden things" to him as the "son" who alone truly knows the Father (11:25-27).[71]

As these examples illustrate, for Matthew the "Son of

---

[71] On this key text for Matthew's christology, cf. J. Dunn, *Christology in the Making*: A New Testament Inquiry into the Origins of the Doctrine of the Incarnation (Philadelphia: Westminster, 1980), 198-202; and M. J. Suggs, *Wisdom, Christology and Law in Matthew's Gospel* (Cambridge: Cambridge University, 1970), 77-97.

God" title highlights Jesus' extraordinary power and his intimacy with God. In Jewish thought the title was a messianic title as well, referring to the king's special role as God's "son," so designated through coronation as leader of Israel (see, for example, the words of Psalm 2, a royal coronation hymn: "You are my son, this day I have begotten you"). It could also refer to the exemplary Israelite, king or otherwise, who suffered trial and torment yet remained faithful to God. This theology of the "suffering just one" is found in some of the psalms and in some chapters of the book of Wisdom. As we will see, Matthew uses this tradition to interpret the meaning of Jesus' death.[72] To these traditional connotations of the "Son of God" title, early Christian tradition had added new layers of meaning. Jesus was the embodiment of Israel's messianic hopes; he was the truly just and obedient Israelite. But he was also one imbued with special divine authority and power and enjoyed extraordinary intimacy with God his father. Through the resurrection Jesus was revealed as the exalted one who had triumphed over death and stood at the right hand of God. All of these layers of meaning are woven into the "Son of God" title when the Gospels apply it to Jesus.[73]

The High Priest's question, therefore, summarizes major assertions of the Gospel about Jesus' identity. As he had in response to Judas' question at the supper (26:25), Jesus replies by bending the spotlight back on the very terms the questioner has used: "*You* have said so".[74] He immediately adds a startling prophecy: "But I tell you, hereafter you will see the Son of Man seated at the right hand of Power, and coming on the clouds of heaven" (26:64)

The parallel to the Caesarea Philippi scene is striking.

[72] Cf. below, pp. 134-135.

[73] See M. Hengel, *The Son of God* (Philadelphia: Fortress, 1976), especially, 57-66.

[74] Matthew is no less affirmative about attributing these titles to Jesus than is Mark (whose parallel, 14:62, has an unequivocal: "I am"); Matthew's phrase — "You have said so" — emphasizes the fact that the truth is contained in the very words Caiaphas puts to Jesus. A similar reply will be given to Pilate in 27:11. On Matthew's phrase, cf. further discussion above, 26:25, p. 64.

There, too, Jesus had supplemented Peter's confession of him as "Christ" and "Son of God" with reference to the *Son of Man's"* coming in triumph and judgment (cf. 16:27-28). As in Mark's Gospel this mysterious title embraces both humiliation and glory.[75] The "Son of Man" has nowhere to lay his head (8:20) and will suffer rejection and death (11:19; 12:40; 17:12, 22-23; 20:18). The very mission of the Son of Man is "not to be served but to serve, to give his life as ransom for the many" (20:28). Yet this same Son of Man, Matthew's Gospel insists, is the one who will come in triumph at the end of the world, gathering together his elect and presiding over the judgment of all humanity (10:23; 13:41; 16:27-28; 24:27, 30, 37, 39, 44; 25:31). Jesus' own mission of healing and forgiveness was a foretaste of that final triumph of salvation (9:6; 12:8).

That mixture of triumph and humiliation is most vividly proclaimed as Jesus stands before his accusers. He is the Son of Man who must be handed over and give his life in service. Yet he is also God's promised deliverer whose faithful death would lead to startling new life. Therefore the Matthean Jesus fearlessly proclaims his full identity to the High Priest. As in Mk 14:62, Jesus' answer is a blend of Ps 110:1 and Dn 7:14, suggesting it was a text formed early in Christian reflection on Jesus' identity.[76] From this very moment the triumph of the Son of Man will make itself felt. He will be seated "at the right hand of Power" (an allusion to Psalm 110 which speaks the exaltation of the king), vindicated by God and reigning with his father in glory. And he will be "coming on the clouds of heaven" (a quote from Dn 7:14) to bring the story of salvation to its completion.

Matthew's version of this saying intensifies the immediacy of Jesus' prediction: "hereafter" or, more literally, "from

---

[75] On the background of this important New Testament title for Jesus, cf. F. Hahn, *The Titles of Jesus in Christology*, 15-53 and J. Dunn, *Christology in the Making*, 65-97. For its use in Matthew, cf. J. D. Kingsbury, *Matthew: Structure, Christology, Kingdom*, 113-22, and B. Lindars, *Jesus Son of Man* (Grand Rapids: Eerdmans, 1984), 115-31.

[76] On this, cf. D. Senior, *The Passion of Jesus in the Gospel of Mark*, 99.

this moment on" these things will be seen.[77] At the instant of Jesus' death Matthew will present awesome signs of the Son of Man's triumph as the earth shakes and the tombs split open (cf. below 27:51-53). Those signs are a foretaste of the Son of Man's triumph over death at the end of the age. Through those signs Jesus' opponents and even more importantly the Christians who encounter Matthew's Gospel will be confronted here and now with the reality of Jesus' exaltation by God. And at the end of the Gospel, the risen Jesus appears in triumph to his disciples on a mountain in Galilee — another sign of the Son of Man's return (cf. 28:16-20).

Jesus' fearless confession of his true identity seals his fate. The High Priest tears his garments, a dramatic gesture of anger at Jesus' "blasphemy." The parade of false witnesses can now be stopped for Jesus' own words make him worthy of death. Note that although the Sanhedrin concurs that Jesus "deserves death" (26:66) they do not yet formally condemn him; the moment of judgment will come early in the morning after a night of interrogation and torment (27:1; contrast Mk 14:64 where the decision is taken during the evening).

Matthew continues to emphasize the hostility of the Jewish leaders against Jesus. It is not simply some bystanders who torment the prisoner (as in Mk 14:65), but the Sanhedrin itself begins to rain abuse on Jesus (26:67-68). He is mocked for his apparent claims to be the Messiah and taunted, "Prophesy to us, you Christ! Who is it that struck you?" For the reader of the Gospel who is not only convinced that Jesus is the Messiah but has witnessed his prophetic knowledge of the approaching events of the passion (see, for example, 26:1-5; 26:17-19; 26:26-29) these taunts have a terrible irony. The Sanhedrin blindly mocks the one who is their Christ and one who knows and accepts the reality of the cup his Father has offered.

[77] Matthew adds a stronger disjunctive "but" at the beginning of Jesus' statement ("But I tell you...") and the adverb *ap' arti* ("from now on") — both of which emphasize the fact that Jesus' dignity as exalted Son of Man will become evident to his hearers. On this cf. B. Lindars, *Jesus Son of Man*, 121; D. Senior, *The Passion Narrative according to Matthew*, 177-83.

PETER'S DENIAL (26:69-75)

Matthew, following Mark, uses a "flashback" technique to pick up the story of Peter, left in suspense since the beginning of the trial (see 26:58). The story of the apostle's failure is one of the most skillfully narrated in the whole Gospel. It stands in obvious contrast with the fearless confession of Jesus before the Sanhedrin. A string of "witnesses" will approach Peter just as they had Jesus; they will accuse him of being "with Jesus" and he will vehemently deny it.

Matthew is consistent in his version of the story. Having eliminated Mark's detail about Peter warming himself at the fire (26:58, compare Mk 14:66) he does so again as he picks up the apostle's story. Peter is sitting "outside in the courtyard with the guards and attendants when a maid comes up to him and accuses him of being "with Jesus the Galilean" (26:69). At several points in the early scenes of the passion story Matthew had stressed the bond between Jesus and his disciples with such a phrase.[78]

Peter's fall will be graceless and mounts in intensity as word of his identity spreads to other bystanders. He immediately denies the maid's accusation, feigning total ignorance of what she means (26:70). Matthew alone notes that the apostle's denial is "before them all." The phrase stresses the public character of Peter's retreat and is identical in wording with earlier significant statements of Jesus about the public witness of discipleship. In the Sermon on the Mount Jesus had challenged the disciples to "let your light shine *before all* (the exact phrase as in 26:70), that they may see your good works and give glory to your father who is in heaven" (5:16). An even more compelling antecedent is found in the mission discourse of chapter 10 where Jesus had warned his followers of the cost of proclaiming the Gospel and had urged them to give fearless witness of their discipleship: "...everyone who acknowledges me *before all,* I will also acknowledge before my father who is in heaven;

---

[78] Cf. 26:18 ("with my disciples"), 26:29 ("with you"), 26:36 ("with them"), 26:38, 40 ("watch with me").

but whoever *denies me before all,* I also will deny before my father who is in heaven" (10:32-33).[79] At the supper table, despite Jesus' warning, Peter had boasted, "Even if I must die with you, I will not deny you" (26:35). Now, unprepared for the crisis, he crumples without struggle at the first encounter with possible danger.

Matthew gives body language to Peter's denial: the apostle retreats from the inner courtyard to the "porch" of the High Priest's residence (26:71). Here a second witness, "another maid," comes forward (contrast Mk 14:69 where it is the same woman who made the first accusation). Now the word begins to spread as she declares to the bystanders, "This man was *with Jesus* of Nazareth." As in the first accusation Matthew continues to focus poignantly on the bond between Jesus and his disciple that is now under assault.

The evangelist also manages to escalate the vehemence of Peter's denials. His evasive claim to ignorance about what his first accuser meant now mounts to an express "oath" denying Jesus: "I do not know the man" (26:72). It is surely not accidental that only Matthew has Peter swear an oath. As we noted above (cf. 26:63) Matthew's Jesus forbids the taking of oaths because it is viewed as a mask for falsehood (5:33-37). From Matthew's point of view, Peter joins an unsavory set of characters whose oaths are signs of their undoing: Herod (14:7), the scribes and Pharisees (23:16-22), and Caiaphas (26:63).

But Peter's tie to Jesus cannot be severed as easily as the apostle wished. Now the bystanders approach him and join in the chorus of accusation, insisting Peter is "one of them" because his Galilean accent betrays his link to Jesus of Nazareth (Matthew makes explicit what is implied in Mark's account; cf. Mk 14:70, "for you are a Galilean"). Sensing that his accusers are mobilizing against him, the beleaguered disciple attempts a fully convincing performance, cursing and swearing, "I do not know the man"

---

[79]The Greek word for "deny," as well as the phrase "before all" are identical to the wording in 26:70.

(26:74). From a mumbled protest of ignorance Peter has moved to a vigorous public denial of his identity as a disciple. Given the role of Peter in Matthew's Gospel this is a moment of intense paradox and tragedy. The very disciple who had unhesitantly proclaimed Jesus as "the Christ, the Son of the living God" at Caesarea Philippi and been blessed by Jesus for his faith, now just as publicly denies that he even knows who Jesus is (compare 16:16-19).

This baffling moment of failure is punctuated by the "cockcrow," the very sign Jesus had predicted at the supper (26:34). [80] That haunting signal penetrates the heart of Peter, and he remembers the words of Jesus warning him of the crisis that lay ahead. His failure reaches its most abject moment: he "went outside and wept bitterly" (26:75). Matthew has worded this differently from Mark (compare 14:72, "he broke down and wept.") The apostle who had vowed never to fall away and who had entered the courtyard of the High Priest determined "to see the end" now retreats "outside," having denied the relationship that gave meaning to his life. He weeps "bitterly," stricken with remorse at the enormity of his failure.

Few scenes draw the Christian reader into the mystery of the passion as this one does. It is obvious that the passion account is calculated not only to retell the sufferings and death of Jesus but to reflect on the crisis that suffering enkindles for those who would follow the way of the Son of Man. In Matthew's passion narrative the denial of Peter is not the only scene in which we follow through on the fate of those who were "with Jesus." At the conclusion of the trial Matthew will also present us with the final chapter of the Judas story (see 27:3-10). This incident, unique to Matthew's Gospel, adds as well a new dimension to the *Peter* story. The failure of the leading apostle not only serves as a foil to the courageous testimony of Jesus but Peter's tears of remorse upon remembering the words of Jesus will contrast with the despair of another apostle who also bitterly regrets his failure but does not choose repentance.

[80]As we noted above (26:34), Matthew has Jesus predict only one cockcrow instead of Mark's two (14:30), and he follows through on that here (contrast Mk 14:72 "...the cock crowed a second time").

JESUS CONDEMNED (27:1-2)

Matthew now switches our attention back to the trial. This mini-scene will bring the proceedings to a formal conclusion. Despite the brevity of the passage the evangelist leaves his distinctive imprint upon it. In Mark's presentation this gathering at daybreak is not part of the formal trial of Jesus but merely a "consultation" (Mk 15:1) in which the Sanhedrin deliberates about handing their prisoner over to Pilate.

For Matthew, however, the Sanhedrin has not yet given a formal verdict on Jesus. When Jesus had boldly declared his identity as the Christ, the Son of God and the triumphant Son of Man, Caiaphas had torn his garments in shocked outrage, and the members of the Sanhedrin had concurred that Jesus "deserved death" (26:66). But their statement was, in Matthew's view, an outburst, similar to the High Priest's dramatic rending of his garments or to the abuse and taunting that the council of leaders heaped on Jesus. It is not yet the final verdict (contrast Mk 14:64 who has the Sanhedrin "condemn" Jesus to death at that very moment). Only at dawn, after the interrogation and mockery and after the episode of Peter's denial, does the end come as the entire Sanhedrin gathers to "take counsel" together.[81] Therefore, for Matthew there are not two sessions of the Sanhedrin (one at night and one at dawn as in Mark) but a night-long trial whose conclusion comes at daybreak.

The net result of all this is to give greater solemnity to the decision the leaders now make: they deliberately choose to put Jesus "to death" (27:1). The silent prisoner is bound and led away to be "handed over" to Pilate the Roman governor (Matthew gives Pilate the formal title he will use frequently in the subsequent scenes). Irony is also at play here. Unwittingly the leaders carry out in exact detail the sequence of events that Jesus himself had predicted. On the road to Jerusalem his prophetic words had focused on this moment: "...the Son of Man will be delivered to the chief priests and scribes, and they will condemn him to death, and deliver

---

[81] Matthew has used this expression several times in his Gospel to describe a gathering of the Sanhedrin in which a decision must be made: cf. 12:14; 22:15; 27:7; 28:12.

him to the Gentiles to be mocked and scourged and crucified..." (Mt 20:18-19). As Jesus is seemingly victimized by
his enemies the reader of the Gospel can also remember the
conclusion to those prophetic words: "...and he will be
raised on the third day."

THE FATE OF THE BETRAYER (27:3-10)

In several passages of the passion story we have noted
Matthew's special interest in Judas. That interest climaxes
here in a scene unique to Matthew: the disciple who had
betrayed Jesus compounds his sin by despair. The full tragic
fate of this doomed disciple now comes to light, as Jesus had
predicted.

But Matthew's interest in this scene is not confined to the
forbidding example of Judas. In fact the thread that runs
throughout this scene is the blood money which Judas had
received from the leaders (26:14-16) and which he now flings
back at them in a vain effort to shed his guilt. The leaders
pick up the money and decide not to put it in the Temple
treasury but to use it to purchase a burial plot for strangers.
The Old Testament fulfillment quotation that closes the
passage (27:9-10) focuses on this strange transfer of the
thirty silver coins. The money seems to be symbolic of the
responsibility Jesus' opponents bear for his death; try as
they might, the money returns to haunt them.

Even though this story is found only in Matthew it does
have some significant parallels to the account of Judas'
death in Acts 1:15-20. In both versions Judas comes to a
violent end that is interpreted as God's judgment on his
betrayal. And in both there is an explanation given for the
name "Blood Field." But there are also great differences on
almost every other point of the story. In Acts the field is
bought *by Judas* with his betrayal money and not by the
Jewish leaders as in Matthew. In Acts Judas seems to die as
a result of an accident, not by suicide as in Matthew. And,
finally, the origin of the name "Blood Field" has a different
explanation in each account: because it is soaked with
Judas' own blood in Acts; because it is purchased with
blood money in Matthew. The differences suggest that a
rather vague tradition about Judas' tragic fate was some-

how connected with the "Blood Field" near Jerusalem, but the exact reasons why had been lost. Each evangelist develops the story in a manner fitting his Gospel.

Matthew is also guided by leads that his source Mark has already given him. At the last supper Jesus had predicted that the disciples would deny, desert, and even betray him and that the betrayer would meet a tragic fate (Mk 14:21; compare Mt 26:24). Mark had followed through in presenting the flight of the disciples at the moment of the arrest and Peter's denial during the trial; in each case Matthew had followed the lead of his source. But Mark does not follow through on Judas; his fate is predicted but not described. Matthew uses the tradition about the Blood Field, reinforced with his typical interest in the Old Testament, to shape the story we are now considering and thereby to complete the scenario predicted but not fulfilled in Mark.[82]

The pace of the story is swift. Judas sees that Jesus is condemned by the formal decision of the Sanhedrin (27:1), and that triggers remorse for his betrayal (27:3). In this opening verse of the passage Matthew has skillfully merged the Judas story into the flow of the passion account. Judas is presented as being in a position to actually see the proceedings against Jesus (thus drawing a parallel to Peter who also is close by the trial room). Matthew's choice of words is deliberate: Judas is described as "having remorse." This is not the word usually used for "repentance" in the Gospels.[83] Stricken by the enormity of his crime he goes back to the chief priests and elders to return the thirty pieces of silver (cf. 26:14-16).

Matthew continues to put the enemies of Jesus in a bad light; if anything, they appear more callous and cynical than Judas. He confesses his crime: "I have sinned in betraying

---

[82] For further discussion of this, cf. D. Senior, *The Passion Narrative according to Matthew*, 346-52; on the death of Judas also see W. C. van Unnik, "The Death of Judas in Saint Matthew's Gospel," *Anglican Theological Review* (Supplementary Series 3; 1974) 44-57, and A. Upton, "The Potter's Field and the Death of Judas," *Concordia Journal* 8 (1982) 213-19.

[83] Matthew is the only New Testament author to use the term *metameletheis* which connotes a change of mind or decision (cf. Mt 21:29, 32); it does not have the almost technical religious meaning of the Greek word *metanoiein* or "repent."

innocent blood." Judas' distraught words sound the major theme of the passage. In the blistering discourse of chapter 23 Jesus had accused the leaders of being responsible for the "just blood" of the prophets from the "innocent" Abel to Zechariah (23:35). Later Pilate would declare that he, in contrast to the leaders and the people who were demanding the crucifixion of Jesus, was "innocent of this man's blood" (27:24).[84]

But the leaders are not moved by their go-between's remorse. They rebuff his attempt to dissolve his pact with them: "What is that to us? See to it yourself" (27:4). Again Matthew's sense of irony is at play here. The words of the Sanhedrin to Judas echo what Pilate will say to them at the moment Jesus is condemned: "I am innocent of this man's blood; *see to it yourselves*" (27:24). In the perennial pattern of human crime those responsible for Jesus' death futilely attempt to wipe his innocent blood from their hands.

Judas' despair is now complete. Rejected by the priests and elders he casts the blood money into the temple and goes to his despairing death. The reader attuned to biblical history might think of Ahithophel, betrayer of David the king, whose fate was suicide by hanging (2 Sm 17:23).

The story of the blood money is not complete. Ironically even though the leaders had rejected Judas' offer to return the silver, they now touch it themselves (27:6). Their statement that it is "not lawful" to put the coins into the Temple treasury "since they are blood money" drives home Matthew's consistently negative portrayal of the leaders. Their concern with legality is mocked by their admission that the money is tainted by the blood of betrayal. They decide to use the money to buy a burial field for strangers. At this point Matthew links his story with the name "Blood Field," a tradition apparently known to his own community (see the remark "to this day" in 27:8).

The rather strange twist of this story comes into sharper focus with the Old Testament fulfillment text that Matthew appends: "And they took the thirty pieces of silver, the price of him on whom a price had been set by some of the sons of

---

[84] Cf. the discussion of this unique Matthean passage below, pp. 116-22.

Israel, and they gave them for the potter's field, as the Lord directed me" (27:9-10). The evangelist asserts that the story of Judas' fate and the collusion of the leaders fulfill a prophecy of "Jeremiah." [85] However, the text Matthew quotes seems to be an adaptation not of Jeremiah but Zechariah 11:13, "Then the Lord said to me, 'Cast it into the treasury' — the lordly price at which I was paid off by them. So I took the thirty shekels of silver and cast them into the treasury in the house of the Lord."

This verse from Zechariah follows immediately upon the text Matthew had alluded to earlier when Judas had sealed his bargain with the priests (cf. above 26:14-16). Zechariah's story of the true shepherd who rejects the slave wages given to him seems to have no sense connection to Judas' story other than the brute description of taking thirty pieces of silver and casting them into the Temple treasury. And in the original quotation there is no mention at all of "the potter's field." Matthew seems to have freely adapted the Zechariah quotation to fit the Judas story and then assigned it to Jeremiah. In Jeremiah 19 there is a long passage in which the prophet is instructed to buy a "potter's" ceramic flask and go to the valley of the sons of Hinnom. There in the presence of the "elders" and "chief priests" he was to break the flask as a sign of judgment upon Jerusalem because of their sins, one of which is that they have "filled this place with the blood of innocents" (Jer 19:4). Because of this prophetic sign the valley is no longer to be called Topheth or valley of the sons of Hinnom but "valley of slaughter" (Jer 19:6) and it will become a burial place (Jer 19:11). [86]

Matthew, therefore, evokes the name and mood of Jeremiah to head these words from the Scriptures. Judas had

[85] Note that here and in 2:17 (referring to the slaughter of the children in Bethlehem) Matthew carefully words his introduction to the fulfillment text; it does not read "in order to fulfill" (as is the case in all the other instances of these quotations) but "*then* was fulfilled . . .". In these two instances the events are tragic and evil; Matthew's subtle wording seems to imply that these events fall under the broad canopy of God's providence but they are not part of God's direct intentionality.

[86] Other passages are appealed to in Jeremiah by some scholars: for example, Jeremiah 32:6-9 which speaks about the purchase of a field or 18:2-3 where the "potter" is introduced. But only in Jeremiah 19 are there so many parallels to Mt 27:3-10. Cf. the discussion in D. Senior, *The Passion Narrative according to Matthew*, 352-62.

betrayed his call to discipleship. His sin was compounded when the staggering guilt of his crime washed over him, but instead of repenting and turning back to Jesus he turned again to the chief priests and elders. From the Gospel's perspective the outcome of such a course could only be rejection and despair. Judas' fate is in stark contrast to that of Peter. Both apostles failed their master but Peter chose repentance and Judas chose death. Matthew also previews the fate of the leaders in this passage. They, too, share in the guilt of the blood money.

For both Judas and the leaders, Jeremiah's prophecy of judgment applies. Their actions fall mysteriously within the span of God's providence. But they are also freely responsible for their unrepentant sin. Just as Jeremiah had warned the city and its leaders of impending doom, threatening that God would break them "as one breaks a potter's vessel" (Jer 19:11), so Matthew is convinced that the destruction of Jerusalem is ultimately a consequence of the choices Judas and his collaborators have made.[87] The function of the Judas story in the passion narrative, however, is not simply to point the finger of judgment at Jesus' past enemies. Matthew knows that the reader of the Gospels is forced to reflect on the consequences of every disciple's choice when confronted with the lure of wealth and the crisis of the passion.

V. Trial Before Pilate (27:11-31)

The passion drama now moves one step closer to its denouement: Jesus stands before Pilate the Roman governor. The Roman trial has particular importance for Matthew's theology; here the Jewish leaders, and ultimately the people themselves, will make their fateful decision about Jesus. As a result sacred history will turn on its axis. There are three episodes in this segment of the passion story: an interrogation of Jesus by Pilate (27:11-14); the choice

---

[87] Cf. a discussion of this aspect of Matthew's theology, below, Part III, pp. 177-81.

between Jesus and Barabbas (27:27-31); the mocking of Jesus by the Roman garrison (27:27-31).

[11]Now Jesus stood before the governor; and the governor asked him, "Are you the king of the Jews?" Jesus said, "You have said so." [12]But when he was accused by the chief priests and elders, he made no answer. [13]Then Pilate said to him, "Do you not hear how many things they testify against you?" [14]But he gave him no answer, not even to a single charge; so that the governor wondered greatly.

[15]Now at the feast the governor was accustomed to release for the crowd any one prisoner whom they wanted. [16]And they had then a notorious prisoner, called Barabbas. [17]So when they had gathered, Pilate said to them, "Whom do you want me to release for you, Barabbas or Jesus who is called Christ?" [18]For he knew that it was out of envy that they had delivered him up. [19]Besides, while he was sitting on the judgment seat, his wife sent word to him, "Have nothing to do with that righteous man, for I have suffered much over him today in a dream." [20]Now the chief priests and the elders persuaded the people to ask for Barabbas and destroy Jesus. [21]The governor again said to them, "Which of the two do you want me to release for you?" And they said, "Barabbas." [22]Pilate said to them, "Then what shall I do with Jesus who is called Christ?" They all said, "Let him be crucified." [23]And he said, "Why, what evil has he done?" But they shouted all the more, "Let him be crucified." [24]So when Pilate saw that he was gaining nothing, but rather that a riot was beginning, he took water and washed his hands before the crowd saying, "I am innocent of this man's blood; see to it yourselves." [25]And all the people answered, "His blood be on us and on our children!" [26]Then he released for them Barabbas, and having scourged Jesus, delivered him to be crucified.

[27]Then the soldiers of the governor took Jesus into the praetorium, and they gathered the whole battalion before

him, [28]And they stripped him and put a scarlet robe upon him, [29]and plaiting a crown of thorns they put it on his head, and put a reed in his right hand. And kneeling before him they mocked him, saying "Hail, king of the Jews!" [30]And they spat upon him, and took the reed and struck him on the head. [31]And when they had mocked him, they stripped him of the robe, and put his own clothes on him, and led him away to crucify him.

THE INTERROGATION BY PILATE (27:11-14)

Matthew begins the trial by quickly introducing the reader back into the flow of the story, a flow diverted by the account of Judas' death and the disposal of the blood money (27:3-10). Previous to that Jesus had been handed over to Pilate by the Sanhedrin (27:2); now that moment flashes back on the screen as Jesus stands as a prisoner on trial before the Roman governor (27:11).

That image of Jesus on trial recalls an earlier point in the Gospel when Jesus had warned the disciples that in the pursuit of their mission they could expect to be "delivered ...up to councils...and...dragged before governors and kings for my sake, to bear testimony before them and the Gentiles'" (10:17-18). First Jesus himself would experience such persecution and then would come the turn of the "members of his household" (10:24-25).[88]

Pilate's opening question poses a major issue of the Roman trial: "Are you the king of the Jews?" As noted above, Jesus' identity as the royal Messiah, the king of Israel, has been no secret in Matthew's Gospel.[89] Following the lead of Mark's account, the title used by Pilate is "king of the *Jews*," instead of the more religiously toned "king of *Israel*." It will be used again as the soldiers mock Jesus (27:29) and will be the charge placed on the cross (27:37). Significantly it was the title on the lips of the magi as they came seeking Jesus: "Where is he who has been born king of

[88]Cf. above, Part I, on passion of the community, pp. 40-45.
[89]Cf. above, 26:64.

the Jews?" (2:2). In each instance the term "Jews" represents the vantage point of Gentiles (Pilate, the soldiers, the magi); when Jewish people use the royal title it is "king of Israel" (see, for example, 27:42).

Jesus' answer seems somewhat enigmatic: "You have said so" (27:11; the same as Mk 15:2). It is probably to be understood as a confirmation of what Pilate has said. Similar to Jesus' response to Judas at the Last Supper (see 26:25) this phrase affirms that the questioner himself has stated the truth in the very question posed. Pilate has not asked "Who are you?" but "Are you the king of the Jews?" Jesus' answer has the touch of irony that runs through the passion story: Jesus' opponents often stumble onto an ironic truth apparent to the reader but hidden from them. Jesus is indeed the "king of the Jews," the son of David longed for by Israel. But like petulant children in the marketplace, Jesus' own generation would fail to recognize him because their expectations did not coincide with the wisdom of God (cf. 11:16-18).

That interpretation seems confirmed by the subsequent verse. The chief priests and elders begin to heap up accusations against Jesus but to them he will give no answer. In this instance there is no explicit truth in their accusations to affirm. Matthew stresses Jesus' silence more than the parallel in Mark does; despite their chorus of charges, "he made no answer" (compare Mt 27:12-14 and Mk 15:3-5). The evangelist does not explicitly quote from the Suffering Servant song of Isaiah but clearly wraps the figure of Jesus in the mantle of that mysterious Israelite who bore abuse in silence and atoned for the sins of the people.

The interrogation closes with Pilate's amazement at Jesus (27:13-14). Despite the governor's encouragement that he answer the charges made against him, Jesus refuses to respond, "not even to a single charge," a point rammed home in Matthew's formulation (27:14; compare Mk 15:5). Such unusual behavior causes the Roman to wonder "greatly." Matthew may have in mind a similar passage in Isaiah (52:14-15):

> As many were astonished at him — his appearance was so
> marred, beyond human semblance, and his form beyond
> that of the sons of men — so shall he startle many nations;
> kings shall shut their mouths because of him; for that
> which has not been told them they shall see and that
> which they have not heard they shall understand. [90]

Earlier in the Gospel Matthew had explicitly portrayed
Jesus as the Servant of Yahweh. His healing power fulfilled
the promise of Is 53:4; the Servant of God was one who
"took our infirmities and bore our diseases" (Mt 8:17). And
his gentle, humble compassion fulfilled another Servant
promise proclaimed in Is 42:1-4:

> Behold, my servant whom I have chosen, my beloved
> with whom my soul is well pleased. I will put my Spirit
> upon him, and he shall proclaim justice to the Gentiles.
> He will not wrangle nor cry aloud, nor will anyone hear
> his voice in the streets; he will not break a bruised reed or
> quench a smoldering wick; til he brings justice to victory;
> and in his name will the Gentiles hope. (See Mt 12:17-
> 21) [91]

That gentle healer is now embodied in the prisoner who
stands silently before Pilate. His absorption of the violent
abuse of his captors will bring new life to God's people. The
stirring of uncomprehending awe in the Gentile governor is
a clear signal for the reader of the Gospel that, despite his
victimization, Jesus' ultimate triumph is certain.

JESUS OR BARABBAS: THE FATEFUL CHOICE (27:15-26)

For Matthew, the most important episode in the trial
scene is the choice that is now about to be posed to the
leaders and the people. The Gospel refers to a custom of

---

[90] The same Greek word *thaumatizein* ("to wonder," "be startled," "amazed") is
used in both Is 52:15 and Mt 27:14.

[91] On the servant image in Matthew, cf. above, Part I, pp. 32-35.

releasing a prisoner of the crowd's choice on the occasion of the Passover feast (27:15). There is no real historical evidence for such a custom other than this report in the Gospels. It may have been a concession on the part of the Romans, attempting to soothe Jewish sensibilities on this liberation feast of the Passover.

In any case, this custom (already reported in Mk 15:6) provides an important device by which Matthew can further amplify a motif that has run throughout his Gospel. Those confronted by Jesus and his message must ultimately choose either to accept or reject him. John the Baptist had sent his disciples to Jesus to pose the key question: "Are you he who is to come, or shall we look for another?" (11:3). All along the course of Jesus' ministry people had either chosen to follow him or oppose him. Chief among the latter had been the Jewish leaders.[92] When the crowds had marveled at his great healings, they judged that "he casts out demons by the prince of demons" (9:34). Instead of recognizing the "deeds of the Christ" (11:2) they had rejected Jesus as "a glutton and a drunkard, a friend of tax collectors and sinners" (11:19). When the crowds had rung out their hosannas as Jesus entered the Temple and purified it, the priests and scribes glowered with indignation (21:15).

Now those many choices to reject Jesus would be forged into a final "no." Throughout this episode of the trial Matthew will highlight that decision by a series of subtle additions and changes in the account of his source. In the opening verse (27:15), for example, he adds the phrase, "whom they wanted." Likewise Pilate's initial question is framed so that both options are clear: "Whom do you want me to release for you, Barabbas or Jesus who is called Christ?" (27:17; compare Mk 15:9, "Do you want me to release for you the king of the Jews?"). The effort of the leaders to sway the crowd again states the clear choice: "...to ask for Barabbas and destroy Jesus" (27:20; contrast Mk 15:11, "...to have him release for them Barabbas instead"). And Pilate restates the decision again in 27:21, "Which of

[92] Cf. Part I, pp. 35-40.

the two do you want me to release for you?" (a question not found in Mark's parallel).

Other features of the text also underscore the element of choice. Only Matthew includes the curious incident of Pilate's wife (27:19). She approaches Pilate to plead for Jesus "the just one" because she had been disturbed about him in a dream. This cameo appearance has the earmarks of Matthew's style. In the biblical world dreams were an important medium of divine messages, and Matthew had introduced a number of them in the infancy narrative. Joseph had learned of Jesus' divine origin through a dream (1:20) and twice had been guided to protect the infant Messiah in dreams (2:13, 19-20). The magi, too, had been warned in a dream not to return to Herod to report their discovery of the newly born king in Bethlehem (2:12). The dream of Pilate's wife is another divine signal about Jesus' true identity.

She calls him a "just" man. As noted above, the word *dikaios* or "just" has particular importance for Matthew's portrayal of Jesus.[93] He is indeed the "just" one who obediently fulfills the demands of God's justice (3:15). This Gentile woman recognizes Jesus' identity and pleads on his behalf, while at the same time the Jewish leaders persuade the crowd to choose Barabbas and destroy Jesus (27:20). Once again in the Gospel the "outsider" proves more perceptive than the "insider," a point that not only advances Matthew's continuing polemic with Pharisaic Judaism but stands as a warning for the Christians who now are the "insiders" of God's people.

It is possible that Matthew has also stressed the element of choice in the very name he gives Barabbas. Some ancient manuscripts have not simply "Barabbas" but "Jesus Barabbas" in 27:17. It is difficult to determine whether a later scribe added the name "Jesus" to dramatize the choice or whether it was part of the original and then later piously eliminated as too scandalous. The latter possibility seems

<hr>

[93] Cf. above, Part I, pp. 26-30.

more probable.[94] In this case the question of Pilate would be: "Whom do you want me to release for you, Jesus Barabbas or Jesus who is called the Christ?" (27:17). That formulation seems to be assumed in Pilate's later question in verse 22 when he asks, "Then what shall I do with Jesus *who is called Christ?*".

The leaders' response to this choice is not in doubt. But the decision of the crowd has yet to be made, and it is here that the drama of the Roman trial scene takes on particular force. Throughout his Gospel Matthew has presented the "crowds" as at least neutral and often favorable to Jesus' mission.[95] They "follow" Jesus and press close to him (4:25; 8:1; 14:13; 19:2; 20:29). They are "astonished" at the power of his teaching (7:28) and give glory to God when he forgives and heals the paralytic (9:8). In contrast to the Pharisees' judgment that Jesus casts out demons through the power of Satan, the crowds marvel and exclaim, "Never was anything like this seen in Israel" (9:33-34). When a blind and mute man is cured by Jesus the crowd inches toward recognizing Jesus as the Messiah, "Can this be the Son of David?" (12:23, again in contrast to the Pharisees who accuse Jesus of being possessed, 12:24). Acclamations of wonder and praise continue as Jesus' mission moves through Galilee and on to Jerusalem (15:31), climaxing in the procession that brings Jesus into the Temple with the crowds shouting their hosannas to the "Son of David" and "the prophet Jesus from Nazareth of Galilee " (21:8, 9, 11, 46).

This neutral, even positive, stance of the crowds toward Jesus has remained as the passion story begins. It was fear of the crowds and their reverence for Jesus that had checked the plot of the leaders until Judas had come forward (21:45-46; 26:5). Up to this point in the story Jesus' opponents were the leaders not the masses. Now that would change,

---

[94] The third century writer Origen states that a number of manuscripts with this unusual reading were known to him. For a fuller discussion of this variant reading, cf. D. Senior, *The Passion Narrative according to Matthew*, 240-41.

[95] Cf. further, P. Minear, "The Disciples and the Crowds in the Gospel of Matthew, "*Anglican Theological Review* (Supplementary Series 3; 1974) 28-44. D. Senior, *The Passion Narrative according to Matthew*, 149-50.

although Matthew continues to lay the blame before the leaders. They are the ones who at the very moment Pilate's wife pleads for Jesus' life "persuade" the crowds "to ask for Barabbas and to destroy Jesus" (27:20). The sway of the crowds away from Jesus seems to be without a struggle: the ringing hosannas (21:9) quickly become "let him be crucified" (27:22, 23).

Matthew, in fact, presents this scene in such a way that the passive crowd, under the pressure of the leaders, is driven to the brink of riot, forcing Pilate's hand. Mark simply says that Pilate wished "to satisfy the crowd" (Mk 15:15) whereas in Matthew the governor sees "that a riot was beginning" (27:24). The increasing frenzy of the crowd and their relentless demand that Barabbas be freed and Jesus be destroyed lead to Pilate's dramatic gesture signaling the verdict and ending the trial. He takes water and washes his hands in sight of the crowd as a sign that he is innocent of the blood of the prisoner he is about to deliver to their will. They catch the meaning of the gesture as they shout back: "His blood be on us and on our children" (27:24-25).

These verses are unique to Matthew's Gospel and are important to his theology. But they are also a New Testament text used repeatedly in Christian history to validate the most vicious forms of anti-semitism. [96] It is important that we examine them carefully and understand them in the context of Matthew's Gospel. [97]

Pilate's symbolic action, taking water and washing his hands before the crowds while declaring his innocence, does

---

[96]Cf. G. Baum, *Is the New Testament Anti-Semitic?* (Glenn Rock, NJ: Deus [Paulist], 1965; F. Lovsky, *Antisemitisme et mystère d'Israel* (Paris, 1955), who cites many examples; E. Flannery, *The Anguish of the Jews* (New York: MacMillan, 1965); J. Fitzmyer, "Anti-semitism and the Cry of 'All the People' (Mt. 27:25)," *Theological Studies* 26 (1965) 667-71. J. Pawlikowski, *What Are They Saying about Christian-Jewish Relations?* (New York: Paulist, 1980), 1-32. The latter gives most attention to the Johannine passion story, however.

[97]For studies on this scene, cf. J. Fitzmyer, "Anti-semitism and the Cry of 'All the People,'" 667-71; J. Quinn, "The Pilate Sequence in the Gospel of Matthew," *Dunwoodie Review* 10 (1970) 154-77; D. Senior, *The Passion Narrative according to Matthew*, 219-62; G. Sloyan, *Jesus on Trial* (Philadelphia: Fortess, 1973), 84-88; W. Trilling, *Das Wahre Israel: Studien zur Theologie des Matthäus-Evangeliums* (STANT 10; München: Kösel-Verlag, 3rd rev. ed., 1964), 66-74.

not seem to be a Roman custom but is drawn from the Old Testament. Chapter 21 of the book of Deuteronomy describes the ritual to be performed when an innocent man is slain and the murderer has not been identified. The leaders of the villages surrounding the scene of the crime are to come together and to break the neck of a heifer. In the presence of the priests the elders are to wash their hands over the slaughtered heifer and to swear their innocence and that of their clan by declaring: "Our hands did not shed this blood, neither did our eyes see it shed (Dt 21:7). Echoes of this same type of ritual are found in the Psalms: "I wash my hands in innocence, and go about thy altar, O Lord.... Sweep me not away with sinners nor my life with bloodthirsty men, men in whose hands are evil devices, and whose right hands are full of bribes" (Ps 26:6-10). Isaiah excoriates the leaders using similar imagery: "When you spread forth your hands, I will hide my eyes from you; even though you make many prayers, I will not listen; your hands are full of blood. Wash yourselves; make yourselves clean; remove the evil of your doings from before my eyes..." (Is 1:15-16).

It is significant that in each of these examples the hand-washing ritual is not simply a declaration of innocence but a plea for repentance and forgiveness. The text of Deuteronomy, which seems to be the major influence on Matthew, is a case in point. The elders' declaration of innocence is followed by this prayer: "Forgive, O Lord, thy people Israel, whom thou hast redeemed, and set not the guilt of innocent blood in the midst of thy people Israel; but let the guilt of blood be forgiven them." At the conclusion of the prayer the text continues, "So you shall purge the guilt of innocent blood from your midst, when you do what is right in the sight of the Lord" (Dt 21:8-9).

The response to Pilate's ritual is also drawn from biblical symbolism. The words "his blood be on us and on our children" echoes a number of Old Testament texts in which someone accepts responsibility for their actions.[98] It has the

---

[98] Cf. H. Kosmala, "'His Blood on Us and on Our Children" (The Background of Matt. 27, 24-25)," *Annual of the Swedish Theological Institute* 7 (1968-69; Leiden, 1970), 94-126.

ring of technical legal language in Leviticus (see, for example, Lv 20:9-16). Other examples are scattered throughout the Hebrew Scriptures. The spies who hid in Rahab's house on the eve of Israel's invasion promise her protection. Anyone in her household who foolishly ventures out of the house will have his "blood upon his head" but if they stay in Rahab's protected house and are still harmed then in that case, the spies declare, their "blood shall be on our heads" (Jos 2:19-20). The same formula is used by David when he declares that the Amalekite deserves death for slaying Saul (I Sm 1:16).

Of particular significance for the text in Matthew are instances in which the formula expresses "collective" guilt for innocent blood. The murder of Abner and Amasa, both "just" men, brings condemnation to the house of Joab: "So shall their blood come back upon the head of Joab and upon the head of his descendants for ever..." (I Kgs 2:33). In a text with striking parallels to the passion story, Jeremiah warns the "princes [of Israel] and all the people" who plot against his life because of his prophetic ministry: "Only know for certain that if you put me to death, you will bring innocent blood upon yourselves and upon this city and its inhabitants, for in truth the Lord sent me to you to speak all these words in your ears" (Jer 26:15).

The Old Testament backdrop for the words and gestures of Pilate and the people in 27:24-25 suggest that this unique material was shaped by the evangelist himself to draw out the meaning of the fateful decision to crucify Jesus. It is no longer simply "the crowds" who speak but "the people" (27:25). The Greek word *laos* or "people" is used some fourteen times in Matthew's Gospel and consistently has a collective sense; that is, not just a crowd but the people of Israel as a whole.[99] Now leaders and crowds have melded into one and form "the people" for whom Jesus was sent and whose sins he was destined to redeem (1:21, "...he will save

---

[99] See, for example, 1:21 (the name "Jesus" is given because he will "save his *people* from their sins") or in the fixed expression the "elders of the *people*" (which occurs five times in Matthew); cf. further, D. Senior, *The Passion Narrative according to Matthew*, 258-59.

his people from their sins"). While Pilate attempts to wipe his hands clean of Jesus' innocent blood the people accept responsibility for it: "His blood be on us and on our children" (27:25).

How does Matthew understand these chilling words? Several layers of meaning seem to converge here. First of all, Matthew interprets the rejection and death of Jesus by Israel as another example of the rejection of the prophets.[100] The theme of "innocent blood" provides an important clue to this. Judas had hurled the silver coins back at the priests, regretting that he had sinned "in betraying innocent blood" (27:4). The priests, in turn, had taken the money and bought the potter's field with it rather than put it in the treasury for they recognized it was "blood money" (27:6). Now both priest and people, the whole nation, accept responsibility for this "innocent blood."

Earlier in the Gospel Jesus himself had connected the motif of "innocent" or "just" blood with the rejection of the prophetic messengers God had sent to Israel. In stinging words Jesus had pronounced an oracle of woe on the scribes and Pharisees, implicating them in the blood of the prophets and warning that "all the righteous blood" of the prophets from Abel to Zechariah would come upon them (23:35). Although "blood" is not explicitly mentioned, the parable of the vineyard, where the tenants reject and kill first the messengers of the owner and finally his son, also interprets Jesus' death in line with this motif (see 21:33-43).

Thus on one level of meaning, Matthew interprets the death of Jesus in line with the death of the prophets. The leaders and people reject and destroy Jesus just as Israel had rejected God's messengers so many times in the past. This was part of the turbulent love story between Yahweh and Israel, a recurring cycle of violent rejection and impassioned reunions. The words of Jesus that conclude the woes of chapter 23 are in this spirit: "O Jerusalem, Jerusalem, killing the prophets and stoning those who are sent to you! How often would I have gathered your children together as a hen

[100]On this motif, cf. above, Part I, pp. 25-26.

gathers her brood under her wings, and you would not! Behold your house is forsaken and desolate. For I tell you, you will not see me again, until you say, 'Blessed is he who comes in the name of the Lord' " (23:37-39).

This motif should not be forgotten when interpreting the meaning of Matthew's passion story. On this level, at least, Matthew's words cannot be understood as anti-Jewish or anti-semitic. The theme they proclaim is itself an ancient Jewish story: God's graciously offered message of love and forgiveness is paradoxically rejected. Such rejection leads to judgment but also to repeated offers of forgiveness when Israel comes to its senses and accepts God's mercy.

But there is more to Matthew's message. From the Gospel's vantage point Jesus is not simply another prophet but God's Son. He comes to Israel as its Messiah and Savior. Therefore the rejection of Jesus is not simply a variation on a theme but a critical choice that would change the course of salvation history. The death and resurrection of Jesus was the turning point of history.[101] The new and final age of salvation had begun. Through its rejection of Jesus and his message Israel had lost an exclusive claim to be God's people; now that privilege would be thrown open to people who would "produce the fruits" of God's vineyard (see 21:43).

In Matthew's perspective this historic choice of Israel was a critical moment, a *kairos*, that brought both judgment and grace. Judgment because the Gospel would move away from Israel and turn to a people who would be responsive. Matthew's community apparently believed that Israel's tragic loss would find historical expression in the destruction of city and temple under the Romans in A.D. 70. That terrifying verdict seems to be expressed in the parable of the vineyard when the owner comes and destroys the tenants because of their infidelity (21:40-41) and in the parable of the banquet when the king punishes those who reject his invitation and murder his messengers (22:7). Jesus himself

[101] Cf. above, Part I, pp. 38-40 and below, pp. 181-84.

had predicted that in the final days not one stone of the Temple would be left standing (24:2).

This interpretation may leave its imprint on the very formulation of 27:25. The people accept responsibility for the death of Jesus on themselves "and on our children." Unlike other instances of the responsibility formula the guilt does not extend "forever" (compare I Kgs 2:33) but only for one generation. From the vantage point of Matthew's community that would mean from the generation contemporary with Jesus down to those who experienced the horrors of the revolt and the destruction of the city in A.D. 70. While not erasing all the shock of this text it makes Matthew's intended meaning a far cry from the perpetual brandmark of responsibility for the death of Jesus that some Christians have imposed on the Jewish people on the basis of this passage.

Would punishment for Israel's sin be terminal? Would Israel no longer be offered the good news of salvation? Some interpreters of Matthew think that is the evangelist's perspective. The rejection of Jesus and the turn to the Gentiles means a definitive loss for Israel.[102] But such may not be the case and Matthew may be closer than is usually admitted to the thought of Paul for whom the promises made to Israel can never be revoked (cf. Rom 11:29 and the whole context of chapters 9-11). Even though the Gospel of Matthew severely reproaches Israel for its rejection of Jesus and the Christian mission, there still seems to be the possibility of repentance. In the discourse of chapter 23 where criticism of the leaders of Israel is most strong, there comes the telling verse: "For I tell you, you will not see me again, *until* you say, 'Blessed is he who comes in the name of the Lord'" (23:39). When Israel recognizes the Messiah it has rejected then it will experience God's mercy.

---

[102] See, for example, D. Hare and D. Harrington, "'Make Disciples of All the Gentiles' (Matt 28:19)," *Catholic Biblical Quarterly* 37 (1975) 359-69. A view contested in the response of J. Meier, "Gentiles or Nations in Matt 28:19?" *Catholic Biblical Quarterly* 39 (1977) 94-102. See also further discussion of the issue in his study *The Vision of Matthew: Christ, Church and Morality in the First Gospel* (Theological Inquiries; New York: Paulist, 1979), 15-17.

But the tragic moment of Israel's rejection is also a paradoxical moment of grace. From Israel's failure would be born the Christian mission to the Gentiles. At the very moment the "children of the kingdom" are cast outside there will come many "from east and west" to sit at Abraham's table (8:11'12).[103] From the "death" caused by Israel's sin would come the new life of the Gentiles' inclusion. Death and resurrection continue to be the deep pattern of the passion story.

There is little doubt that the Roman trial scene and its climactic choice by the people is an integral part of Matthew's theology of history. It bears as well scar tissue from the friction between the Jewish Christian community and Pharisaic Judaism. Both dimensions must be kept in mind if this controversial, and dangerous, biblical text is to be interpreted in a responsible way.[104]

The choice made, the scene concludes with a terse statement: "Then he released for them Barabbas and having scourged Jesus, delivered him to be crucified" (27:26). The lash of irony is again felt. The people receive what they asked for, a notorious criminal (27:16), while their true king and savior is brutally scourged and handed over to death. The verdict is a devastating commentary on their choice.

MOCKERY OF THE KING (27:28-31).

The Roman trial ends with Jesus tortured and mocked by Pilate's soldiers. This final episode of the trial parallels the ending of the hearing before the Sanhedrin (26:67-68). There Jesus had been mocked as the "Christ," a major concern of the Jewish trial; here he is mocked as "the king of the Jews," the very title Pilate had asked of Jesus at the opening of the Roman trial (27:11). In each episode the strong irony of the passion story is at work.

Matthew follows Mark closely here but has introduced

---

[103]On this point cf. D. Senior and C. Stuhlmueller, *The Biblical Foundations for Mission* (Maryknoll: Orbis, 1983), 246.

[104]Cf. further discussion of this below, Part III, pp. 181-184.

some intriguing changes. The mockery and torture are a cruel interlude between the decision of Pilate (27:24-26) and the march to Golgotha. At the end of the trial Pilate had handed over Jesus to be scourged prior to crucifixion but that punishment is not described; instead we have a scene of torment and derision.[105] Matthew tends to emphasize even more than Mark the parody of kingship inflicted on Jesus.

The "whole battalion" (at full strength, almost 600 men) gathers before Jesus. They proceed to a mock coronation and then a ceremony of mock homage. The "king of the Jews" is stripped naked and given a "scarlet" robe. Mark mentions a "purple" robe, the color worn by the emperor (Mk 15:17). Scarlet was the color of the ordinary Roman soldier's outer tunic. Matthew's detail is not only more probable historically but may be intended to intensify the level of mockery (parallel to a reed for a sceptre and thorns for a crown). He is given a crown of thorns for his royal diadem and a stick for a sceptre. Matthew alone mentions this latter part of the investiture; Mark will note that the soldiers strike Jesus on the head with a reed (15:19) and this may have suggested the detail of the mock sceptre to Matthew.

Once the "king" has been given his royal robes the soldiers begin to offer mock homage, a game that soon escalates into violence, as they move from acclamations to spitting and blows. It is interesting that Matthew has reordered the various elements of this mockery to give the scene a pattern of escalating violence: kneeling, acclamation, spitting, striking (compare Mk 15:18: acclamation, striking, spitting, kneeling). In a Gospel that strongly recoils from violence this act of brutality takes on additional meaning. The use of violence runs directly counter to the teaching of Jesus, as Matthew had already indicated at the moment of the arrest (cf. above 26:52-54).

---

[105] Here is another example of the notable restraint of the Gospels concerning the physical agonies of Jesus. In contrast to some of the classical martyrdom accounts of Judaism and early Christianity, the passion narratives do not linger over the physical torments of Jesus but seem to concentrate more on the theological significance of his suffering.

Their violence spent, the soldiers divest Jesus of his "royal" robes and give him back his own clothing (only to be stripped again at the crucifixion, cf. 27:35). The meaning of this violent and cruel episode is found in the soldier's mocking acclamation: "Hail, king of the Jews!" (27:29). The trial scene ends as it began: Pilate had opened his interrogation with the question, "Are you the king of the Jews?" (27:11). And Jesus' identity as the "Christ," the royal anointed Messiah of Israel, had been the leitmotif of the entire trial (see 27:17, 22). The leaders, the entire people, and now the Romans all reject Jesus' claim.

But the Christian reader catches the supreme irony of the mock coronation. Jesus is rejected but in the very mode of the rejection his true identity as king of Israel and king of the Gentiles is paradoxically proclaimed. Not only is Jesus truly a king, he is a king in a manner totally different from those "rulers of the Gentiles" who exercise their authority in "lording it over the others" (20:25). Herod had been oblivious to this reality at the very beginning of the Gospel. When he heard of one "born king of the Jews" (2:2) he feared a rival claimant to his power and was driven to deceit and murder. In contrast to Herod and his Jerusalem court, the magi had recognized Jesus' true royal dignity. Similarly the soldiers mock Jesus because they see him as a weak and helpless pretender to the only kind of royal authority they have experienced. The reader knows that in their parody of the trappings of royalty there lies an irony much different from what the soldiers intend. Jesus, in fact, is not at home with such symbols of power — not because he lacks royal status but because his power is that of the Son of Man, who came "not to be served but to serve, and to give his life as a ransom for many" (20:28).

VI. Crucifixion and Death (27:32-56)

The trial concluded, the passion story now races to its awesome finale. The scene shifts from the praetorium inside the city to Golgotha, the place for public executions outside the walls of Jerusalem.[106] As has been the case throughout the passion narrative, Matthew's account is close to that of Mark. But in these climactic scenes more than anywhere else Matthew has made some dramatic changes in the narrative of his source.

This section of the passion falls into two major episodes: Jesus is crucified and exposed to a final mockery (27:32-44) and then death comes with thunderous drama (27:45-56).

> [32]As they went out, they came upon a man of Cyrene, Simon by name; this man they compelled to carry his cross. [33]And when they came to a place called Golgotha (which means the place of a skull), [34]they offered him wine to drink, mingled with gall; but when he tasted it, he would not drink it. [35]And when they had crucified him, they divided his garments among them by casting lots; [36]then they sat down and kept watch over him there. [37]And over his head they put the charge against him, which read, "This is Jesus the king of the Jews." [38]Then two robbers wre crucified with him, one on the right and one on the left. [39]And those who passed by derided him, wagging their heads [40]and saying, "You who would destroy the temple and build it in three days, save yourself! If you are the Son of God, come down from the cross." [41]So also the chief priests, with the scribes and elders, mocked him, saying, [42]"He saved others; he cannot save himself. He is the king of Israel; let him come down now from the cross, and we will believe in him. [43]He trusts in God; let God deliver him now, if he desires him; for he said, 'I am the Son of God.'" [44]And the robbers who were crucified with him also reviled him in the same way.

---

[106] Historians continue to debate the probable location of the Roman trial. Some would locate the scene at the Antonium fortress adjacent to the Temple where sizeable numbers of Roman troops were quartered. Others prefer what is known as the "citadel" near the present day Jaffa Gate, the site of Herod's fortified Jerusalem residence. The more regal accommodations available at this site suggest that it, not the Antonium, would have been the residence of the Roman procurator when he came from Caesarea Maritima to Jerusalem for festivals or other state business.

45Now from the sixth hour there was darkness over all the land until the ninth hour. 46And about the ninth hour Jesus cried with a loud voice, "Eli, Eli, lama sabachthani?" that is, "My God, my God, why hast thou forsaken me?" 47And some of the bystanders hearing it said, "This man is calling Elijah." 48And one of them at once ran and took a sponge, filled it with vinegar, and put it on a reed, and gave it to him to drink. 49But the others said, "Wait, let us see whether Elijah will come to save him." 50And Jesus cried again with a loud voice and yielded up his spirit. 51And behold, the curtain of the temple was torn in two, from top to bottom; and the earth shook, and the rocks were split; 52the tombs also were opened, and many bodies of the saints who had fallen asleep were raised, 53and coming out of the tombs after his resurrection they went into the holy city and appeared to many. 54When the centurion and those who were with him, keeping watch over Jesus, saw the earthquake and what took place, they were filled with awe, and said, "Truly this was the Son of God!" 55There were also many women there, looking on from afar, who had followed Jesus from Galilee, ministering to him; 56among whom were Mary Magdalene, and Mary the mother of James and Joseph, and the mother of the sons of Zebedee.

CRUCIFIXION AND FINAL MOCKERY (27:32-44).

Led by Pilate's soldiers, Jesus is taken outside the city to Golgotha (27:32). The location of Jesus' execution "outside" had already been alluded to in the parable of the vineyard where the wicked tenants cast the son "out of the vineyard, and killed him" (a detail special to Matthew, 21:39). The death of Jesus outside of Jerusalem seems to capture that abject rejection of the Messiah that so commands Matthew's attention in this part of the Gospel.

As the execution detail moves along it happens upon Simon, a stranger from Cyrene (a city in northern Africa in what is modern-day Libya), perhaps a diaspora Jew visiting Jerusalem for the Passover. The soldiers force Simon to carry the cross of Jesus. Matthew eliminates the bit of information supplied by Mark, namely that Simon was "coming in from the countryside" and that he was "the father of Alexander and Rufus" (Mk 15:21). Some have suggested that because it was a feast day Matthew's Jewish sensibilities may have omitted the reference to Simon's having been in the countryside. But there is no sure indication that by referring to the countryside (literally, the "field") Mark implies that Simon was at work. More than likely Matthew eliminated this and the bit of information about "Alexander and Rufus" as superfluous details, a reaction typical of his style throughout the Gospel.[107] Simon's brief appearance is not embroidered by Matthew, but it would be hard for the Christian reader not to think of Jesus' saying earlier in the Gospel: "If anyone would come after me, let him deny himself and take up his cross and follow me" (16:24).

The description of the moment of crucifixion is swift. They arrive at "Golgotha" or "the place of the skull" (27:33). Neither Matthew or Mark explain the significance of the name; it is not clear whether "skull" referred to the location's notorious use as an execution site or to its physical shape. Here the prisoner is offered a mild narcotic to help deaden the pain of crucifixion. Jesus tastes but does not drink it. Matthew's description of the drink as wine "mingled with gall" (27:34) clearly links this moment to Ps 69:22, "They gave me poison (translated in the Septuagint as *choles* or "gall," the same Greek word Matthew uses) for food, and for my thirst they gave me vinegar to drink." Immediately before his death the other part of this psalm verse would be fulfilled when one of the bystanders offers Jesus "vinegar" to drink (see 27:48).

This entire psalm is a prayer of "lament," a brutally honest prayer in which the psalmist cries out to God in the midst of torment and isolation:

---

[107] This aspect of Matthew's style is documented in the classic work of J. C. Hawkins, *Horae Synopticae: Contributions to the Study of the Synoptic Problem* (Oxford: Clarendon Press, 2nd rev. ed, 1909), 158-60.

> Save me, O God! For the waters have come up to my
> neck. I sink in deep mire, where there is no foothold; I
> have come into deep waters, and the flood sweeps over
> me. I am weary with my crying; my throat is parched. My
> eyes grow dim with waiting for my God. . . . Thou know-
> est my reproach, and my shame and my dishonor; my
> foes are all known to thee. Insults have broken my heart,
> so that I am in despair. I looked for pity, but there was
> none; and for comforters, but I found none. They gave
> me poison for food, and for my thirst they gave me
> vinegar to drink (Ps 69:1-3, 19-21).

As we will discuss below, the mood of the biblical lament
suffuses this entire section of the passion story.[108] Jesus
"fulfills" the Scriptures not only through his powerful words
and actions but also in his union with the sufferings of the
just ones of Israel who had faithfully endured the testing of
their faith.[109]

The actual moment of crucifixion is quickly stated in a
subordinate clause, without a single detail of description
(27:35). In none of the Gospels is there any interest in the
gory details of Jesus' sufferings. Crucifixion was undoubtedly a brutal form of execution; the Romans reserved it
almost exclusively for slaves and lower classes, especially
for crimes of sedition.[110] Despite the dramatic potential of
dwelling on the physical torment involved in Jesus' crucifixion, the Gospels give their attention to the meaning rather
than to the gruesome aspects of this event. Subtle allusions
to the Scriptures, the statements of the mockers, and Jesus'
own dying prayer command the attention of the passion

---

[108] Cf. below, 27:45-56.

[109] As in Mark, portrayal of Jesus as the suffering Just One is an important part
of Matthew's theology of the passion. On the background of this motif in the Old
Testament, cf. L. Ruppert, *Jesus als der leidende Gerechte?* (Stuttgarter Bibelstudien 59; Stuttgart: Katholisches Bibelwerk, 1972).

[110] On this cf. M. Hengel, *Crucifixion* (Philadelphia: Fortress, 1981); J. Fitzmyer, "Crucifixion in Ancient Palestine, Qumran Literature, and the New Testament," *Catholic Biblical Quarterly* 40 (1978) 493-513.

account for it is here that the significance of Jesus's death is told.

The garments of an executed criminal became the property of the execution detail, so the soldiers divide Jesus' garments among them (27:35). The passion story undoubtedly alludes here to another important lament, Psalm 22:

"Yea, dogs are round about me; a company of evildoers encircles me; they have pierced my hands and feet — I can count all my bones — they stare and gloat over me; they divide my garments among them, and for my raiment they cast lots" (Ps 22:16-18).

This magnificent Old Testament prayer in its entirety has a major role in the passion narratives of Mark and Matthew.[111] In addition to the reference to the division of garments, such details as the "wagging" of the mockers' heads (27:39), Jesus' claim to be "God's Son" (27:43), and his dying words (27:46) are all drawn from this haunting prayer of faith and anguish. It is also possible that the very structure of Psalm 22 has had an influence on the crucifixion and death scenes, especially in Matthew's account. Similar to many of the lament prayers, Psalm 22 moves from cries of anguish and desolation in the first part of the psalm (22:1-21) to a triumphant sense of God's fidelity in the last half of the prayer, as Yahweh listens to and vindicates the trust the Just One of Israel has placed in him (22:22-31). In Psalm 22 this vindication portion of the psalm ecstatically declares that God's trustworthiness will be recognized by "the ends of the earth" and "all the families of the nations" (Ps 22:27-28).

---

[111]Cf. L. R. Fischer, "Betrayed by Friends, An Expository Study of Ps. 22," *Interpretation* 18 (1964) 20-27; H. Gese, "Psalm 22 und das Neue Testament. Der Alteste Bericht vom Tode Jesu und die Entstehung des Herrenmahles," *Zeitschrift für Theologie und Kirche* 65 (1968) 1-22 (a digest in English is found in *Theology Digest* 18 [1970] 237-43); H. D. Lange, "The Relationship between Psalm 22 and the Passion Narrative," *Concordia Theological Monthly* 43 (1972) 610-21; J. Reumann, "Psalm 22 at the Cross," *Interpretation* 28 (1974) 39-58; D. Senior, "A Death Song," *The Bible Today* 14 (1974) 1457-75; D. Senior, "The Death of God's Son and the Beginning of the New Age (Matthew 27:51-54)," in A. Lacomara (ed.), *The Language of the Cross* (Chicago: Franciscan Herald Press, 1977), 29-52.

Even "all who go down to the dust" will bow in homage before God, a probable allusion to sheol, the shadowy abode of the dead.[112]

This movement of the psalm from lament to vindication, as well as its strong emphasis on the psalmist's trust in God even in the midst of torment and the vindication of that trust by God, are deeply entwined with the motifs that run through this section of the passion story. Although the psalm had already influenced Mark's version (and probably accounts of Jesus' death before Mark's Gospel was written) Matthew has extended the influence of the psalm in his portrayal of Jesus' crucifixion, mockery, and death. As we shall discuss below, Matthew's passion story will stress both Jesus' trust in God and the cosmic vindication of that trust in the acclamation of Gentiles and the stirrings of life in the abode of the dead (27:51-54).

Their prisoner impaled on the cross, the Roman soldiers sit down "and keep watch over him" (27:36). Matthew emphasizes this attentive presence of the soldiers which adds a note of expectancy (contrast Mk 15:25 where no mention is made of the soldiers taking up a position of watching). When Jesus had been led before the Sanhedrin, Peter had "sat down" with the guards in the courtyard "to see the end," preparing the reader for the drama of his denial (26:58). Later the faithful women, who witness the crucifixion and burial of Jesus and who will be the first to encounter the Risen Christ, will take up a similar vigil, "sitting opposite the tomb" (27:61). The soldiers who sit by the cross of Jesus will witness the explosion of events at the moment of his death and will be the first to acclaim that the crucified Jesus is the triumphant "Son of God" (notice that Matthew makes an explicit connection to this earlier verse by describing them as those "who were . . . keeping watch over Jesus," 27:54).

A placard is fixed to the cross over Jesus' head stating the

---

[112]The Hebrew text of the psalm is poorly preserved and difficult to translate at this point; on this cf. C. Stuhlmueller, *Psalms*, Vol. 1 (Old Testament Message 21; Wilmington: Michael Glazier, 1983), 150, who defends this basic reading.

charges against him (27:37). Matthew makes this moment a formal declaration of Jesus' identity: "This is Jesus the king of the Jews" (contrast Mk 15:26, "The king of the Jews"). Again irony rises to the surface of the passion story. What the soldiers do in derision of a crucified Jew becomes a proclamation of Gospel truth. This man impaled on the cross is, by the very act of giving his life, worthy of the name "Jesus," the one who "will save his people from their sins" (1:21). This man hoisted on the tree of death is by that sacrifice enthroned as "king of the Jews," the messianic liberator of God's people.

Two "robbers" or "insurrectionists" (the term *lestai* used here could mean either) are crucified with Jesus, one on his right and the other on his left (27:38). This entourage of death continues the macabre and ironic parody of Jesus' royal status. His court is composed of outcasts and evil-doers, the very thing he was accused of by the leaders (see, for example, 11:19: "a friend of tax collectors and sinners").

A procession of taunters now begins to flow past the cross. Matthew again alludes to Ps 22 (see 27:39) by noting the arrogant "wagging" of their heads as they hurl their words toward Jesus: "All who see me mock at me, they make mouths at me, they wag their heads..." (Ps 22:7). Jesus embodies this great prayer of Israel in this moment of the passion. He is alone among his tormenters, abandoned by everyone he loved. Only that tenacious faith in God that had driven him throughout his ministry and been rekindled in Gethsemane would sustain him now.

The mockers' words probe and test that faith. An assertion of the trial is brought back: "You who would destroy the Temple and rebuild it in three days, save yourself!" (27:40; compare 26:61). Power over the Temple was a messianic prerogative; now the one alleged to have claimed that power is pinned helpless to a cross. That paradox is the thrust of the mockery; the messianic pretender who would assume to destroy the Temple is now challenged to save himself. Once again the irony is intense. Matthew's reader who moves through this story from the perspective of resurrection faith and with the searing memory of the Temple's destruction catches the unwitting truth of the mockers' words. The Temple, in Matthew's perspective, would indeed be destroyed because of Jesus' death. And the challenge to "save yourself" also finds paradoxical realization not by escape from the cross but in the very moment of crucifixion. Jesus had taught his disciples that "whoever would save his life will lose it, and whoever loses his life for my sake will find it" (16:25).

The first set of mockeries is rammed home with a phrase found only in Matthew: "*If you are the Son of God*, come down from the cross" (27:40; compare Mk 15:30). A foreboding memory stirs from early in the Gospel. Fresh from his baptism in the Jordan and ready to plunge into his mission of justice, the Christ had encountered Satan in the desert (4:1-11). The demon's attempts to turn Jesus aside from his mission had begun with the same mocking words: "If you are the Son of God..." (cf. 4:3, 6). And each time the Spirit-filled Jesus had thrust aside Satan's test by reasserting his obedience to God's word.[113] Now the demonic lure has been cast at Jesus again, as the very opponents who had accused Jesus of being in league with Satan (cf. 9:34; 12:24) themselves parrot the demon's proposals. Instead of being asked to turn stones into bread or to cast himself from the Temple or to worship Satan (in exchange for the kingdoms of the world) the offer now is to "come down from the cross."

All of these tests are the same: to pull Jesus aside from the way God had set, to seek his own aggrandizement and his own rescue at the expense of giving himself for others. Unlike the desert scene, Jesus would make no reply other than remaining on the cross. His unyielding commitment to God's word had already been expressed in Gethsemane as the armed mob encircled him and his disciples had been tempted to take up the sword. He would refuse violence and take up the cross for if he should do otherwise, "how then should the Scriptures be fulfilled, that it must be so?" (26:54).

---

[113]On this scene in Matthew and its connection to the passion story, cf. B. Gerhardsson, *The Testing of God's Son* (Lund: C. K. Gleerup, 1966), 7-83.

A second set of mockers now came on the scene, the "chief priests, with the scribes and elders" — the entire Sanhedrin who had condemned Jesus — process by him and taunt him. The historical improbability of this should be obvious. The intent of the Gospel is clearly not to describe the actual details of Jesus' final moments of life but to bring forward the issues and storms of conflict that have surrounded Jesus' ministry of justice from the beginning.

The leaders' mockeries begin with words similar to those of the "passersby" (cf. 27:40): "He saved others; he cannot save himself." The words are undoubtedly an ironic paraphrase of Jesus' own teaching in 16:25 (cited above) only in saving others could Jesus "save" himself. The word "save" has deep and comprehensive meaning in Matthew's Gospel; it refers to the total transformation and redemption of the human person, body and spirit.[114] As such it catches the very purpose of Jesus' entire mission: he had come to "save" people from their sins (1:21). Twice in Matthew the disciples had implored that their "Lord" would "save" them (8:25; 14:30).

Another accusation of the trial is dredged up and hurled at Jesus: "He is the king of Israel; let him come down now from the cross, and we will believe in him." (27:42). Pilate had made Jesus' identity as the "king of the Jews" the capital issue of the Roman trial.[115] The leaders use the more religious designation "king of *Israel*" as they deride Jesus' messianic claim and once again make separation from the cross a litmus test for belief in him.

The reader who has followed Matthew's story from the beginning and has seen the repeated and explicit teaching of Jesus on the necessity of the cross catches the full contradiction of the leaders' request. Twice before in the Gospel they had demanded spectacular "signs" from Jesus to authenticate his mission (12:38; 16:1). Each time Jesus had refused and left them with the promise of only one "sign," the "sign

---

[114]The word is used fourteen times in Matthew, in each ease implying deliverance from harm; in addition to the examples cited in the text, cf. 9:21, 22 (twice); in 10:22; 19:25; 24:12, 22 it refers to final salvation.

[115]Cf. above 27:11-26.

of Jonah" who had spent three days and three nights in the belly of the whale. That sign of dying and rising would be the only authenticating evidence of Jesus' messiahship. But it was a sign the leaders could not comprehend.

The final words of mockery are found only in Matthew: "He trusts in God; let God deliver him now, if he desires him; for he said, 'I am the Son of God'" (27:43). Once again the evangelist draws on Psalm 22 to shape the spirit and content of the passion story. The psalmist laments that he is surrounded by mockers who taunt him: "He committed his cause to the Lord; let him deliver him, let him rescue him, for he delights in him!" (Ps 22:8).

But there is another Old Testament passage that may also influence Matthew's text. The early chapters of the book of Wisdom also use the device of mockery to put in bold relief the tenacious faith of the "Just One" who trusts in God despite torment and the threat of death.[116] The mockers ridicule the Israelite's claim to be a "child of the Lord" and suggest that a "shameful death" (Wis 2:20) would be a good way to test such trust. At this point the author of Wisdom seems to expand on the elements of mockery in Psalm 22 and, in fact, quotes from the earlier psalm the exact verse used by Matthew: "Let us see if his words are true, and let us test what will happen at the end of his life; for if the righteous man is God's son, he will help him, and will deliver him from the hand of his adversaries" (Wis 2:18; cf. Ps 22:8).

This final mockery in which even the two robbers crucified with Jesus join brings to the surface the basic issue of the passion story. Throughout the Gospel Jesus has been proclaimed as God's Son, as the Davidic Messiah sent to liberate Israel and to establish justice.[117] The angel had reassured Joseph that the child Mary bore was "conceived... of the Holy Spirit" (1:20). The voice from heaven had ratified that divine sonship at the Jordan as Jesus had

---

[116] On the influence of the Book of Wisdom in the New Testament passion accounts, cf. B. Beck, "'Imitatio Christi' and the Lucan Passion Narrative," in W. Horbury and B. McNeil (eds.), *Suffering and Martyrdom in the New Testament* (Cambridge: Cambridge University, 1981), 43-44; D. Senior, *The Passion Narrative according to Matthew*, 288-90.

[117] Cf. above, Part I, pp. 26-30.

accepted John's baptism of repentance and inaugurated his messianic mission (3:17). The same voice would do so again on the mountain of transfiguration (17:5). Less awesome but still important voices had recognized Jesus as God's Son when the disciples had worshipped him in the boat (14:33) and Peter had confessed him as the "Christ" and the "Son of the Living God" at Caesarea Philippi (16:16). Jesus himself had affirmed it by his repeated address to God as his "Father" in prayer (see, for example, 6:9; 11:25; 26:39, 42) and, above all, in the loving fidelity to God's will that is a hallmark of the Matthean Jesus.[118]

With daring intuition the Gospel of Matthew makes this fundamental commitment of Jesus the issue in question at the moment of death. Jesus becomes *"the* Israelite," *"the* believer," buffeted, torn, face to face with the most unnerving mystery of life. The words of the mockers give voice to death's fiercest threat: can the bond of love and trust that ties Jesus to his God and God to Jesus be broken by death? That is the challenge the mockers hurl at the "Just One" in the Book of Wisdom. That is the anguished question that gives birth to the lament of Psalm 22. And that is the probing question that coexists with all authentic faith. Is God's love more powerful than death? As the passion moves to the climactic scene of Jesus' own encounter with death, it is this awesome question that hangs in the air over Golgotha.

THE DEATH OF GOD'S SON (27:45-56).

The passion drama now moves to its great crescendo. It is high noon (the "sixth" hour) and a brooding darkness settles over Golgotha, lasting until three o'clock (the "ninth" hour, 27:45).[119] The reader attuned to the biblical world will no

---

[118] The importance of the titles "Son" and "Son of God" is stressed by J. Kingsbury in his analysis of Matthew's christology; cf. *Matthew: Structure, Christology, Kingdom*, esp. pp. 40-83.

[119] Matthew seems to give less attention than Mark to the chronology of the passion. In 27:36 (compare Mk 15:25) he had omitted the reference to the "third hour" at the time of the crucifixion and in 27:46 he will note "*about* the ninth hour" (compare Mk 15:34).

doubt think of the darkness threatened for the end of time, as humanity witnesses the passing of the old age and feels the "birth pangs" of the new. Jesus had painted such a vision of chaos when telling his disciples of the end of the world: ". . . the sun will be darkened, and the moon will not give its light, and the stars will fall from heaven, and the powers of the heavens will be shaken" (24:29).

Many commentators believe that in this opening verse of the death scene Matthew (following the lead of Mark, 15:33) alludes to Am 8:9, " 'And on that day,' says the Lord God, 'I will make the sun go down at noon, and darken the earth in broad daylight.' " In Matthew's version the precise wording of the phrase "over all the land" is identical to Ex 10:22 where Moses stretches out his hand and a plague of darkness falls "over all the land" of Egypt for three days. In any case, the evangelist has painted a mood of awesome threat; the decisive moment of world history has come and humanity has moved into the eye of the hurricane.

The eerie stillness is pierced by a heart-clutching scream from the man on the cross. And now the psalm that had already provided much of the spirit and content of the final hour of Jesus' life moves again to the fore. Jesus cries out in prayer with Psalm 22 on his lips, Israel's most powerful and naked lament.[120] Matthew presents the opening line of Psalm 22 first in Hebrew — *Eli, Eli, lama sabachthani?* — and then in translation for his Greek-speaking readers, "My God, my God, why hast thou forsaken me?"[121]

By making this prayer the death prayer of Jesus the evangelist catches up the motif of trust and vindication already raised in the mockery scene (cf. 27:32-44). Even though shredded by anguish Jesus, the Just One, prays a prayer of raw, unadorned faith in God. As he had from the very beginning of the Gospel, Matthew presents Jesus as the embodiment of Israel's faith, as the one who suffers with

---

[120]On the role of this psalm in the passion tradition, cf. above, pp. 129-30.

[121]There are many variations in the manuscripts on the precise form of the Hebrew and/or Aramaic text of Matthew here; for details, cf. D. Senior, *The Passion according to Matthew*, 295-96; K. Stendahl, *The School of St. Matthew and Its Use of the Old Testament* (Philadelphia: Fortress, 1968), 83-87.

God's people and yet remains faithful.[122] Only the first line is quoted but the spirit of the entire psalm is at work here. The lament of the psalmist weaves together hoarse cries of pain with tenacious assertions of faith:

> Why art thou so far from helping me, from the words of my groaning? O my God, I cry by day, but thou dost not answer; and by night, but find no rest...

> Be not far from me, for trouble is near and there is none to help....

> But thou, O Lord, be not far off! O thou my help, hasten to my aid!

> Yet thou art holy, enthroned on the praises of Israel. In thee our ancestors trusted; they trusted, and thou didst deliver them. To thee they cried, and were saved; in thee they trusted, and were not disappointed....

> Yet thou art he who took me from the womb; thou didst keep me safe upon my mother's breasts. Upon thee was I cast from my birth, and since my mother bore me thou hast been my God...

The bystanders hear the prayer of the Crucified Jesus and react with what seems to be a final torment. They misunderstand the Hebrew word *eli* (="my God") in Jesus' prayer for the name Elijah. It is difficult to say whether their misunderstanding is presented as deliberate or not. The great prophet Elijah had rescued the widow and her son from starvation and had delivered Israel from danger and idolatry (cf. the story of Elijah in I Kings 17). He was recognized in later Jewish tradition as a kind of "patron saint" of lost causes.[123] This seems to be the interpretation the bystanders give to Jesus' prayer: "This man is calling Elijah" (27:47). One of them runs and fills a sponge with vinegar, puts it on a reed

---

[122]Cf. above Part I, p. 23.

[123] J. Jeremias, "'*El(e)ias*," in G. Kittel (ed.), *Theological Dictionary of the New Testament*, Vol. 2, 930-31.

and offers it to Jesus (thereby another thread of Scripture weaves its way through the scene as Matthew again alludes to Ps 69:21).[124] But others stop the man from offering the wine, preferring to mock Jesus and test the power of his prayer: "Wait, let us see whether Elijah will come to save him" (27:49).[125]

However, the words of the bystanders bring another ironic level of meaning to the scene. They taunt this condemned man who is so obviously discredited and abandoned by God that no salvation is possible for him: ". . . let us see whether Elijah will come to *save* him." (In Mark's parallel the wording is different: ". . . let us see whether Elijah will come *to take him down*" [15:36]).[126] As we noted above, the word "save" is a powerful theological term in the Gospel.[127] Used frequently in the miracle stories it expresses the comprehensive transformation of body and spirit that is the very intent of Jesus' mission. The verb is also used to refer to that final salvation God would bring to Israel in the endtime: the one who endured to the end would be "saved" (cf. 10:22; 24:13, 22). Significantly the same verb is found throughout Psalm 22: "To Thee they cried, and were *saved*" (22:5); "He committed his cause to the Lord; let him deliver him, let him *save* him, for he delights in him" (22:8); "*Save* me from the mouth of the lion, my afflicted soul from the horns of the wild oxen!" (22:21).

Jesus had been an instrument of God's salvation throughout his ministry. In word and healing gesture he had "saved" Israel from its sin and been a living sign of the coming rule of God, the final age of salvation (cf. 12:28). But Jesus as the true Israelite had also *experienced* God's saving love; it was

[124] Cf. above, 27:34, the reference to the "gall" offered to Jesus at the beginning of the crucifixion scene where Matthew highlights an allusion to Psalm 69.

[125] Note that Matthew has clarified the somewhat confused description of Mark at this point. Mark has the "one" who goes to get the sponge of vinegar stop himself (cf. 15:36)! Matthew's version seems to make more sense: one bystander attempts to relieve Jesus' anguish when he cries out, but "others" stop the man from carrying out the gesture.

[126] This wording, too, is quite deliberate and fits into Mark's overall theology where the attempt to separate Jesus from the cross is a major issue of the Gospel. Cf. D. Senior, *The Passion of Jesus in the Gospel of Mark*, 124-25.

[127] Cf. above p. 133, n. 118.

that revelation for which he had thanked his Father (11:25-27) and taught his disciples to do the same (6:6-9). Now Jesus' own body was broken and his own spirit bent by the power of death. The healer needed healing; the savior longed for salvation.

In the darkness of his death struggle the saving love of the Father seemed distant, even denied, and so Jesus cries out with Israel's prayer of deliverance, a prayer that in the paradox of faith both laments God's absence and draws upon his living presence. It is the efficacy of this prayer that the bystanders challenge, ironically preparing for the explosion of events that will give divine validation to the power of Jesus' death prayer.

The bystanders mention Elijah in their taunt of Jesus' prayer and wonder if the prophet will come to save Jesus, but the reader of the Gospel remembers another important truth about Elijah. Elijah is presented as the prophet of the endtime in the New Testament. Matthew's Gospel had explicitly identified John the Baptist as Elijah returned, the prophet who in preparing for the messianic mission of Jesus would usher in the final chapter of world history (11:7-14, esp., 11:14; 17:10-13; also 3:1-6 where John appears in the garb of Elijah).[128] Now signs of that final age inaugurated by John-Elijah and brought to realization by Jesus himself are about to break into the world.

The moment of death comes with stunning quickness, as it so often does. Jesus "cried again" and "yielded up his spirit" (27:50). Matthew has carefully formulated these terse words. In Mark's parallel Jesus appears to die with a wordless scream (15:37); there are no words, no attempt at control or cogency as the Son of Man's life is poured out for the many.[129] But Matthew has subtly changed Mark's stark description. Jesus does not "utter a loud cry" but "cries out again." The verb *kragzas*, "cry out," is the same word used repeatedly in Psalm 22 to describe the desperate prayer of the Just One (cf. Ps 22:2, 5, 24). Of particular significance is

---

[128] Cf. above Part I, pp. 23-26.

[129] For a discussion of this text in Mark, cf. D. Senior, *The Passion of Jesus in the Gospel of Mark*, 125-26.

22:24: "For he has not despised or abhorred the affliction of the afflicted; and he has not hid his face from him, but has heard, when he *cried* to him." Our attention is also called to this psalm by the word "again" in Matthew's text. The first cry of Jesus had broken out in 27:46 when he had prayed the first verse of the psalm; now that lament breaks out "again." Matthew, therefore, gives meaning to the wordless scream of Jesus; Jesus' second cry is the same as the first — he dies with the lament of Psalm 22 on his lips.

The spirit of that prayer also seems to guide Matthew's description of the instant of death: Jesus "yields up his spirit" (contrast Mark 15:37 where Jesus "expires"). The Greek word *pneuma*, "breath" or "life-spirit," used here expresses a Jewish conception of human life. The breath of life is a gift of God, endowed on humankind from the first moment of creation: ". . . then the Lord God formed man of dust from the ground, and breathed into his nostrils the breath of life; and man became a living being"(Gn 2:7). That life-breath, although the vital core of human existence, belongs to God and at the end of each human history must be given back "to God who gave it" (Qoheleth 12:7). [130] Psalm 104 catches this sovereignty of God over all life:

> These all look to thee, to give them their food in due season. When thou givest it to them, they gather it up; when thou openest thy hand, they are filled with good things. When thou hidest thy face, they are dismayed; when thou takest away their *breath*, they die and return to their dust. When thou sendest forth thy *Spirit*, they are created; and thou renewest the face of the ground (Ps 104:27-30). [131]

In "yielding up his life-breath" to God, Matthew's Jesus dies with an act of obedience. That is the same spirit that had

130 The Hebrew term *ruah* ("spirit," "breath"), translated as *pneuma* ("spirit," "breath," "wind," etc.) in the Septuagint is exceptionally rich in connotation; cf. H. W. Wolff, *Anthropology of the Old Testament* (Philadelphia: Fortress, 1974), 32-39.

131 In the Septuagint translation of the psalm both "breath" and "spirit" translate the identical word *pneuma*.

driven Jesus from the beginning of the Gospel story. Matthew's repeated assertion of Jesus' awareness of the approaching passion and his determination to face that *kairos*, his eloquent gestures and words over the bread and the cup, Jesus' urgent prayer of obedience in Gethsemane and the spirit of union with his Father that suffused it, the loyal insistence on "fulfilling the Scriptures" at the moment of the arrest, the fearless confession of his mission before the Sanhedrin and Pilate — all of these elements of the passion story portray Jesus as knowingly and willingly facing the cross in a spirit of reverent obedience to God and to the mission of salvation God had asked of him. Now all of that life-commitment was caught up in a death shout, a prayer of agony and faith. And with the shout a final act of integrity: the sacred life-breath of the Son of God is handed back in trust to the God who had given it.

Such a prayer could not go unanswered. If the spirit of Psalm 22's lament had animated the first part of the crucifixion scene then the spirit of vindication in the latter half of the psalm dominates the conclusion of the scene.[132] At the instant of Jesus' death (note the phrase "And behold," tying the events to the instant of death, 27:51) the earth explodes with a series of awesome signs (27:51-53). These "happenings" (as they are called in 27:54) are all described with the passive tense, implying that it is God who is their author. They are awesome, cosmic signs of God's answer to the prayer of Jesus. With the exception of the tearing of the Temple veil, these "signs" are unique to Matthew's account and reveal his special interpretation of the death of Jesus.[133] In the Greek text of Matthew, the events are all linked

[132]On the structure of the lament, cf. above, pp. 127-30.

[133]On this segment of Matthew, cf. D. Hutton, *The Resurrection of the Holy Ones (Mt. 27:51b-53). A Study of the Theology of the Matthean Passion Narrative* (Unpublished Dissertation; Harvard University, 1970; M. Riebl, *Auferstehung Jesu in der Stunde seines Todes? Zur Botschaft von Mt 27, 51-b-53* (Stuttgarter Bibelstudien 8; Stuttgart: KBW, 1978). Hutton contends that Matthew 27:51-53 (as well as 28:2-3, the appearance of the "Angel of the Lord") is influenced by an apocalyptic account of the resurrection of Jesus that is also reflected in the apocryphal Gospel of Peter. For a different view, cf. D. Senior, "The Death of Jesus and the Resurrection of the Holy Ones, Matthew 27:51-53," *Catholic Biblical Quarterly* 38 (1976), 312-29.

together in a single sentence, beginning with the tearing of the Temple veil, then an earthquake, then the splitting of the rocks and the opening of the tombs, and then the resurrection of the saints and (after Jesus' own resurrection) their appearances to many in Jerusalem (27:51-53). The resurrection of the "holy ones" is the climax toward which the other events lead. Each of the events or signs has peculiar significance and deserve some comment.

The only event with a parallel in Mark's text is the tearing of the Temple veil, "from top to bottom" (27:51). Presumably the veil referred to is the veil that hung before the "holy of holies," setting the boundary for the inner sanctuary, the most sacred area of the Temple, where the ark of the covenant and the manna were kept, and where no Israelite could enter except the High Priest once a year on the feast of Yom Kippur.

The first result of the death of Jesus in both Mark and Matthew is the tearing open of this sacred barrier. Neither evangelist comments on the precise significance of such a striking event. In the case of Mark one can deduce from the rest of the Gospel that this event is primarily a sign of judgment upon the Jerusalem Temple.[134] The actions of Jesus in Jerusalem shortly before his arrest had signaled the condemnation of the Temple; like the fig tree cursed for bearing no fruit, the Temple "made by hands" would be brushed aside for a new and spiritual temple "not made by hands." That temple would be the Christian community itself, open to people of all nations (cf. Mk 11:17).

For Mark, therefore, the tearing of the veil is a sign of judgment upon the Temple "made by hands." With the death of Jesus, God's presence is not confined to the holy of holies but has been made present in the crucified body of Jesus and in the community gathered in his name. The acclamation of the centurion who recognizes Jesus as "the Son of God" (Mk 15:39) confirms this divine manifestation. The tearing of the veil is indeed an "opening," providing new access to God, but for the Temple itself such an "opening" is a sign of condemnation.

[134] Cf. D. Senior, *The Passion of Jesus in the Gospel of Mark*, 126-29.

The significance of the tearing of the Temple veil is similar in Matthew. Although Matthew does not retain Mark's distinction of a Temple "made with hands" and one "not made by hands," and has presented Jesus' actions in the Temple more in the line of a purification rather than a condemnation, his Gospel does foresee ultimate judgment coming upon the Temple in connection with Jesus' death.[135] Matthew and his community apparently interpreted the destruction of the Temple by the Romans in A.D. 70 as divine punishment for the rejection of Jesus and his message.[136]

Equally important, the Temple's destruction is foretold by Jesus as one of the events signalling the coming of the end of the world (24:2). This helps Matthew link the tearing of the veil with the other cosmic signs that follow. As we will point out, all of them are the kind of events Judaism expected for the endtime. Therefore the tearing of the veil not only signals the end of the Temple era — because of the infidelity of God's people — but the inauguration of a new and final age of grace. The demarcation between the old and the new age is the death and resurrection of Jesus. In this sense the tearing of the veil has a positive meaning as well: it is an opening of access, a liberating act that will be chain-linked to other events leading up to the freeing of the dead from their tombs.

The events which follow the tearing of the veil extend the impact of Jesus' death deeper into the earth.[137] The earth shakes and the rocks are split (27:51); both are events asso-

[135] The parable of the vineyard speaks about the kingdom being taken away from the leaders and "given to a nation producing the fruits of it" (21:43); in 23:38 Jesus pronounces a prophetic "woe" upon Jerusalem, predicting that its "house is forsaken and desolate"; in 24:2 Jesus again pronounces a prophecy against the temple: "Truly, I say to you, there will not be left here [i.e., the Temple] one stone upon another, that will not be thrown down."

[136] Cf. our discussion of 27:24-25; also Part III below, pp. 179-81.

[137] Some Jewish traditions compared the Temple veil to the firmament of the heavens. A. Pelletier has suggested this connection may also be at work in Matthew's text, implying an organic unity between the tearing of the veil [=the heavens], the rending of the earth and the opening of the graves — equivalent to one great cosmic opening; cf. "La tradition synoptique du 'voile déchiré' à la lumiere des realites archeologiques," *Revue des Sciences Religieuses* 46 (1958), 162-80.

ciated with the end of the world in the Bible and in Jewish literature of the intertestamental period.[138] Matthew follows this pattern in Jesus' apocalyptic discourse when "earthquakes" are listed as one of the signs beginning the "birth pangs" of the new age (24:8). But Matthew's Gospel also has a "shaking of the earth" happen at other special moments when divine power makes itself felt. In his version of the storm at sea, the catastrophe threatening the disciples and their boat is a great "turbulence" — the Greek word used is *seismos*, the identical root word used to describe the "shaking" of the earth (Mt 8:24; contrast Mk 4:37 who uses the word *lailaps*, an ordinary word for "storm" or "squall"). Jesus then displays his own divine power over storm and sea and rescues the disciples from the threatening chaos.[139] Another "great earthquake" will be felt as an "Angel of the Lord" comes to roll back the stone from the entrance to Jesus' tomb, an event found only in Matthew's Gospel (28:2).

The "splitting of the rocks" prepares for the climactic sign of resurrection. Jesus himself will be laid in a tomb "hewn in the rock" (27:60) and such was a common mode of burial in Israel. The explosive events that now radiate from the obedient death of Jesus are not destructive but liberating, breaking open the rock tombs that hold God's "holy ones."

The resurrection of the just was also a sign of the final age in some Jewish traditions.[140] This expectation is what Matthew invokes as he describes the opening of the tombs and the raising of the bodies of the "holy ones" who had "fallen

---

[138] A number of biblical texts refer to earthquakes accompanying the day of God's visitation: cf., for example, Jgs 5:4; 2 Sm 22:8; Ps 68:8; Ps 104:32; Jl 4:14-17. Splitting of the rocks in connection with God's presence is found in 1 Kgs 19:11; Ps 114:7; Is 48:21 (referring to the splitting of the rock to procure water during the exodus). These motifs are also found in non-biblical Jewish writings of the intertestamental period, for example 4 Ezr 9:2-3; 2 Bar 32:1, 1 En 1:3-9, etc.

[139] Cf. G. Bornkamm, "The Stilling of the Storm in Matthew," in G. Bornkamm, G. Barth, H. J. Held, *Tradition and Interpretation in Matthew* (Philadelphia: Westminster, 1963), 56.

[140] Cf. a full discussion of this issue in G. Nickelsburg, *Resurrection, Immortality, and Eternal Life in Intertestamental Judaism* (Harvard Theological Studies 26; Cambridge: Harvard University Press, 1972).

asleep" (27:52). Two specific Old Testment texts may have influenced Matthew at this point. The book of Daniel concludes its vision of the endtime with this portrayal of final judgment:

> And there shall be a time of trouble, such as never has been since there was a nation till that time; but at that time your people shall be delivered, every one whose name shall be found written in the book. And many of those who sleep in the dust of the earth shall awake, some to everlasting life, and some to shame and everlasting contempt (Dn 12:1-2).

An even stronger influence on Matthew is Ezekiel's dream of the dry bones (Ez 37:1-14). Taken by God to the desert, the prophet sees the wilderness floor littered with dry, bleached bones. Then God breathes his "spirit" into the bones and they come together, taking on sinew and flesh, a resurrected people who then march triumphantly into Israel. Yahweh interprets the dream for Ezekiel:

> Son of man, these bones are the whole house of Israel. Behold, they say, "Our bones are dried up, and our hope is lost; we are clean cut off." Therefore prophesy, and say to them, "Thus says the Lord God: Behold, I will open your graves, and raise you from your graves, O my people; and I will bring you home into the land of Israel. And you shall know that I am the Lord, when I open your graves, and raise you from your graves, O my people. And I will put my spirit within you, and you shall live, and I will place you in your own land; then you shall know that I, the Lord, have spoken, and I have done it, says the Lord" (Ez 37:11-14).

The references to the "opening of graves" and the return of the risen people to Israel have striking parallels to Matthew's portrayal of the raising of the saints. The spirit of both texts are also similar. Ezekiel's vision is a declaration of hope for a people shattered by exile (just as the apocalyptic vision in Daniel was an assertion of ultimate triumph during the dark days of Greek rule in Israel). Yahweh would intervene to breathe new life into their broken hopes, forming them once again into a people and giving them back their land. Archaeological evidence has shown that this striking vision of Ezekiel was later interpreted in a messianic way: the messiah would be the one to infuse God's spirit into the people and lead them to salvation.[141]

That is what Matthew seems to do in alluding to this biblical text in the wake of Jesus' obedient death. Through Jesus' death and resurrection God has effected the final salvation promised to Israel. A new people, built on the "holy ones" who had slept in death awaiting God's redemption, would now be raised up. The hopes that forged Ezekiel's dream of liberation and Daniel's vision of Israel's ultimate triumph are now realized in the final age brought about through Jesus.

One can sense the meaning of a text like this for Matthew's battered Jewish-Christian community. Their mission to Israel had for the most part failed; instead of being united with them in following Jesus as the Christ and Risen Lord, most Jews had followed the leadership of the Pharisees and thought of Matthew's Christians as renegades. And now to compound the anxiety of those Jewish Christians, the community was being flooded with Gentile believers who did not share the sacred heritage and refined religious sense of Judaism. Indeed, Matthew's Christians could have made the words of Ezekiel's haunting dream their own: "Our **bones are dried up, and our hope is lost; we are clean cut off"** (Ez 37:11). By reminding them of Ezekiel's vision of hope renewed and a people risen from their tombs, Matthew

[141]This is apparent in the visual depiction of Ezekiel 37 found in the third century A.D. Dura-Europos synagogue. There the Messiah is depicted standing before the Mount of Olives and breathing the spirit on the dry bones; the newly awakened people march into Jerusalem. On this remarkable fresco, cf. H. Riesenfeld, "The Resurrection in Ezekiel 37 and in the Dura-Europos Paintings" *Uppsala Universitats Arsskrift* 11 (1948) 27-38. R. Wischnitzer-Bernstein, "The Conception of the Resurrection in the Ezekiel Panel of the Dura Synagogue," *Journal of Biblical Literature* 60 (1941) 53-55. A photo of the panel can be found in J. Gutmann (ed.), *The Dura-Europos Synagogue: A Re-Evaluation (1932-72)* (Missoula: SBL/AAR, 1973), 178.

attempted to stir the vitality of his anxious church. By making the death and resurrection of Jesus the fulfillment of that text he recalled for them the foundation of their hope and, at the same time, reminded them of the inevitable pattern of sacred history: from death comes unexpected life.[142]

The essential link between the death-resurrection of Jesus and the beginning of the new age strains Matthew's narration. He wants to show that God's acts of salvation come immediately as a response to the obedient death of Jesus. That final act of Jesus' life is itself redemptive and is the reason for his triumph over death. Matthew attempts to express that theological intuition by having the cosmic signs follow immediately upon Jesus' death rather than wait until Jesus' resurrection and the resulting discovery of the empty tomb. But placing the cosmic signs of God's vindication here also causes theological static. Jesus' own resurrection and his triumphant appearance to his disciples must come first (cf. 28:9-10, 16-20); the basic teaching of the New Testament is that Jesus is the "firstborn," the beloved of God who first tastes victory over death and brings all humanity after him (see, for example, Rom 8:29: I Cor 15:20). Therefore Matthew must insert into his description of the resurrection of the saints the curious qualifier "after his [Jesus'] resurrection" (27:53). Only after Jesus has experienced victory over death and given testimony of that through his appearances to the women at the tomb and to his disciples on a Galilean mountaintop, will those who experience resurrection through him enter the holy city to give their own testimony to God's redemptive power.

This staggering chain of events is witnessed by "the centurion and those who were with him, keeping watch over Jesus" (27:54). The execution detail had been sitting watching the events on Golgotha in an attitude of expectancy (cf. above 27:36). Seeing the "earthquake and the happenings" (the literal meaning of Matthew's words here) the Gentile soldiers are seized with "fear" and acclaim with one voice: "Truly this was the Son of God!"

---

[142]Cf. the discussion of Matthew's "theology of history" below, pp. 181-84.

Matthew has carefully worded this climactive verse to make it a choral ending to the entire crucifixion scene. Once again the mood of Psalm 22 seems to be at work. Jubilant because of God's faithfulness the psalmist had prayed: "All the ends of the earth shall remember and turn to the Lord; and all the families of the nations shall worship before him. For dominion belongs to the Lord, and he rules over the nations" (Ps 22:27-28). In Mark's version the acclamation comes from a single centurion who is the first human being in the Gospel to recognize Jesus as "Son of God" (15:39). But in Matthew there are multiple witnesses, the first of the "families of the nations" who would confess Jesus.

The precise motive for the acclamation is also different in Matthew's version than in Mark's. The centurion in Mark "*sees how he* [Jesus] *died*" (15:39). The manner of Jesus' death becomes a revelation for the centurion; the "weakness" of the crucified Jesus in giving his life totally reveals the power of God, a revelation missed by Jesus' opponents who will "see and believe" only if Jesus comes down from the cross (cf. Mk 15:32).[143] But in Matthew the centurion and his companions are moved to acclamation because they witness the earthquake and the series of cosmic signs that explode at the moment of Jesus' death (note that in Mark the only sign is the tearing of the Temple veil and that seems to be presented as an event not witnessed by the soldiers; cf. Mk 15:38-39). This leads them to "fear greatly," an attitude of religious awe that frequently seizes witnesses of divine signs in the Bible.[144]

These "events," as we have discussed above, are presented by Matthew as God's "answer" to the challenges hurled at Jesus by his opponents. Caiaphas the High Priest had asked Jesus on an oath if he were "the Christ, the Son of God,"

---

[143]On this interpretation of Mark's scene, see D. Senior, *The Passion of Jesus in the Gospel of Mark*, 129-32.

[144] For examples in Matthew, cf. 9:8 (the crowd "fears" and praises God after the cure of the paralytic), 17:6 (the disciples react with fear at the transfiguration), 28:8 (the women leave the tomb in "fear and joy" after encountering the Angel of the Lord).

only to reject Jesus' positive response as "blasphemy" (26:63-66). As he hung on Golgotha Jesus had been taunted by the bystanders to save himself "if you are the Son of God" (27:40). And the Jewish leaders had mocked him in the same way, "He trusts in God; let God deliver him now, if he desires him; for he said, 'I am the Son of God'" (27:43). The reader of the Gospel knows that Jesus is God's Son. The voice from the heavens had declared it so (3:17; 17:5) and the disciples and Peter had confessed their Master's true identity (14:33; 16:16). But now the one endowed with divine power had given his life and hung powerless on the cross; death seemed to have stripped from Jesus his identity as one beloved by God. Death puts all relationships in question and Matthew has presented the final struggle of Jesus precisely in these terms. But the cosmic signs of new life erupting from the grave had vindicated Jesus' trust and proclaimed that God's faithful love could not be overwhelmed, even by death. The awe of the Roman guards and their acclamation of Jesus' enduring sonship are the final comment on the validity of the good news.

Matthew associates with these Gentile witnesses the presence of "many women" who were "looking on from afar" (27:55-56). The Gospel identifies them as those "who had followed Jesus from Galilee, ministering to him" (27:55), a succinct description of faithful discipleship. In Bethany at the very beginning of the passion story an anonymous woman had also stood by Jesus and ministered to him, anointing him for burial over the protests of his other disciples (cf. above, 26:6-13). Now the story comes to its close with another group of those "outsiders" who make brief appearances in the Gospel drama yet seem to exemplify authentic discipleship in a manner that far transcends those with more prominent roles.[145] The apostles and Peter have fled but these remain.

Two of the Marys named will go to the tomb with Jesus' body (27:61) and the day after the Sabbath will be the first to

---

[145] Cf. our discussion of the "unexpected disciples" below, pp. 175-77.

discover the empty tomb and to encounter the Risen Christ (28:1-10). The Son who revealed his Father only to the "lowly" would again confound the "wise and the understanding" (11:25).

VII. Vigil at the Tomb (27:57-66).

The final two scenes of Matthew's passion narrative have a muted atmosphere. After the explosive events surrounding Jesus' death, the burial has a touching, reflective mood (27:57-61). And the continuing efforts of the leaders to thwart Jesus' influence (27:62-66) seem feeble and anticlimactic in the wake of the thunderous signs vindicating Jesus at the cross. Both scenes also serve to project the reader towards the resurrection.

> 57When it was evening, there came a rich man from Arimathea, named Joseph, who also was a disciple of Jesus. 58He went to Pilate and asked for the body of Jesus. Then Pilate ordered it to be given to him. 59And Joseph took the body, and wrapped it in a clean linen shroud, 60and laid it in his own new tomb, which he had hewn in the rock; and he rolled a great stone to the door of the tomb, and departed. 61Mary Magdalene and the other Mary were there, sitting opposite the sepulchre.
>
> 62Next day, that is, after the Day of Preparation, the chief priests and the Pharisees gathered before Pilate 63and said, "Sir, we remember how that impostor said, while he was still alive, 'After three days I will rise again.' 64Therefore order the sepulchre to be made secure until the third day, lest his disciples go and steal him away, and tell the people, 'He has risen from the dead,' and the last fraud will be worse than the first." 65Pilate said to them, "You have a guard of soldiers; go, make it as secure as you can." 66So they went and made the sepulchre secure by sealing the stone and setting a guard.

THE BURIAL (27:57-61)

In his typical style, Matthew's account of the burial is lean and to the point, accomplished by omitting a number of the details found in Mark, such as the rather complex description of the time in Mk 14:42 and the mention of Pilate's wonderment at the quick death of Jesus (15:44-45a).[146] Matthew's version has a different spirit from that of Mark. The one who comes to bury Jesus is not "a respected member of the council" nor is his act of compassion a sign of his search "for the kingdom of God" (see Mk 15:43). In Matthew's account Joseph of Arimathea is a "rich man" and a "disciple" (27:57). Both of these descriptions fit into the evangelist's perspective. Many interpreters of this Gospel have noted a subtle orientation toward the rich, suggesting that Matthew's community may have included wealthy members.[147] Joseph represents a member of the community willing to risk his resources for the sake of one in extreme need, the crucified Jesus who is in solidarity with the "least" (see 25:31-46). For a wealthy person to give an honorable burial to someone publicly rejected by the Jewish authorities and executed by the Romans was at best an imprudent gesture, at worst, dangerous exposure.

The fact that Joseph is a "disciple" and not a member of the Sanhedrin (as in Mk 15:43 and even more explicitly in Lk 23:50-51) continues the sharp cleavage Matthew has drawn between the followers and the opponents of Jesus. The disciples are those who through their deeds courageously minister to their Lord; while the Jewish leaders, exponents of those who have rejected the Gospel, will continue

---

[146]Note, however, that Mark's reference to the "Day of Preparation" (15:42), omitted by Matthew at the beginning of the burial story, will be retrieved to introduce his special material about the placing of the guard in 27:62.

[147]In his Gospel Matthew refers to a whole range of words for coins (much more than Mark) and refers to such terms as "gold," "silver," and "talent" (equal to more than a thousand dollars) some twenty-eight times (compared to only one such reference in Mark and only four in Luke!). On this cf. J. Kingsbury, *Matthew* (Proclamation Commentaries; Philadelphia: Fortress, 1977), 97-98.

their furtive attempts to oppose the Messiah (cf. 27:62-66). Like his namesake at the beginning of the Gospel this Joseph displays his commitment to Jesus not through elaborate words but by decisive deeds. [148]

Joseph goes to Pilate and asks for the body of Jesus. Pilate immediately orders its release. Matthew does not delay over Pilate's amazement at Jesus' rapid death as is the case in Mark (15:44). Instead the focus falls on the act of burial itself. Joseph receives the body (the word used here is the generic term *soma*, the same used at the Last Supper in 26:26; Mark uses the more jarring term, "corpse" [*ptoma*], cf. Mk 15:45) and wraps it in a "clean linen shroud" and places it "in his own new tomb" (27:59-60). The descriptive details "clean"and "new" and the fact that the tomb belongs to Joseph personally are touches found only in Matthew. They follow through on Joseph's status as a "rich" man and continue to show the loving care of this disciple for Jesus.

Having completed the burial, Joseph rolls a "great"stone in front of the door, sealing the tomb, and departs. The size of the stone not only attests to the fitting magnificence of the tomb but also prepares for the subsequent scenes. The chief priests and Pharisees will be anxious to have this tomb sealed even further in their ironic fear that somehow Jesus and his message will escape the shackles of death (27:62-66), and the Angel of the Lord will roll back this very stone and sit on it in triumph after the resurrection (28:2).

Two of the women who had been at the cross (cf. above, 27:55-56), Mary Magdalene and the "other Mary" (presumably the "mother of James and Joseph" mentioned in 27:56) take up their vigil, seated in mourning opposite the tomb (27:61). Their posture is reminiscent of the soldiers who had sat down in front of the cross to keep watch over Jesus (cf. above, 27:36). In each case this silent vigil is a signal of marvelous and startling events about to break across the Gospel stage and overwhelm the witnesses who sit in expectation.

---

[148]Cf. Mt 1:24; 2:14; 2:21. An emphasis on good deeds is a hallmark of authentic discipleship in Matthew's Gospel: cf. above, Part I, pp. 29-30, 36.

SETTING A GUARD (27:62-66).

This incident is found only in Matthew's Gospel, and it serves as an effective contrast with the beautiful example of discipleship in the previous scene. The evangelist continues to portray the leaders as implacable foes of Jesus and his message. Their resolute choice against Jesus solemnly ratified at the Roman trial (27:25) carries beyond the moment of death. The chief priests and Pharisees — the two most prominent groups opposing Jesus during his ministry in Galilee and Jerusalem — go to Pilate to demand that a guard be placed at the tomb. The cast of characters and the tone of the scene are reminiscent of the Roman trial. There, too, the leaders had pressed a seemingly reluctant Pilate to accede to their wishes (cf. above 27:11-26).

It is likely that Matthew himself has composed this scene rather than drawing on specific historical information about this secret meeting.[149] The leaders' assertion that the disciples would steal Jesus' body from the tomb and fraudulently proclaim his resurrection (27:63-64) probably reflects the kind of counter-arguments to Christian preaching Matthew's community had heard from their Jewish contemporaries. That seems to be what the evangelist implies in the follow-up to this story, where the Sanhedrin bribes the guards into claiming the disciples had stolen Jesus' body (cf. 28:11-15). This story, Matthew asserts, "has been spread among the Jews *to this day*" (28:15).

These concluding stories, therefore, present us with two radically different interpretations of the empty tomb. For those Jews opposed to the Christians the empty tomb was a hoax perpetrated by Jesus' disciples. For the Christians it is an act of God, triumphantly vindicating the obedience of his Son.[150]

---

[149]Cf. the discussion of a possible historical foundation for this incident in W. Craig, "The Guard at the Tomb," *New Testament Studies* 30 (1984) 273-81.

[150]As John Meier points out, it is interesting that both interpretations presuppose an *empty* tomb; Matthew's traditions do not suggest that Jesus' body remained in the tomb. Cf. *Matthew* (New Testament Message 3; Wilmington: Michael Glazier, 2nd rev. ed., 1981), 356.

As in the previous scene, this brief story recapitulates earlier events and projects the reader toward the conclusion of the Gospel. The leaders themselves recall Jesus' predictions of his triumph over death (". . . we remember how that impostor said, while he was still alive, 'After three days I will rise again'"), a telling irony as the Gospel stands on the brink of the resurrection story. With another touch of irony on Matthew's part, the leaders also predict that the disciples will proclaim to the people: "He has risen from the dead," a wary anticipation of the great missionary commission that will conclude the Gospel (28:16-20). Even in death the leaders continue to fear Jesus's attraction to the people (cf. above 26:5). They also worry that the "last fraud will be worse than the first" (27:64), another ironic hint of the community's explosive and universal mission that would begin with the death and resurrection of Jesus. If in his earthly ministry Jesus himself had crashed like a titanic wave over Israel, how much more would the Son of Man shake the foundations of the world when he came in triumph and commissioned apostles in his name. Jesus had also warned his disciples that there would be a price to pay for fearlessly proclaiming the Gospel (10:24-25), and ominous hints of that can be found in this opposition, organized now not only against Jesus but against what his disciples will say of him.

Pilate gives in to the request of the leaders, just as he had done in the trial. His words, "go, make it as secure as you can" (literally, "as you know"), may have a twinge of mockery, not impossible for one who is presented as knowing Jesus was delivered up "out of envy" (27:18) and who ceases to resist demands for Jesus' death only after declaring his own innocence (27:24).

The scene ends with the leaders going to the tomb, sealing the stone before the entrance and placing their guard.[151]

---

[151]Some see an allusion to the incident in Dn 6:17 where the king seals the prophet in the lion's den. See, for example, J. Meier, *Matthew*, 358; E. Schweizer, *The Good News according to Matthew* (Atlanta: John Knox, 1975), 521, who notes that the two events were associated in early Christian art.

That ending completes Matthew's preparation for the victorious resurrection scenes. Once again jolting contrast serves the evangelist's dramatic purpose. Two groups surround the tomb of Jesus: on one side are Joseph, who had lovingly ministered to his Master's needs, and the faithful women who take up their expectant vigil; on the other, the Jewish leaders nervously bargaining for more security, leaving in place a guard of uncomprehending soldiers.

The passion story seems to end as it began. As the fateful day had loomed the leaders had plotted in secret against Jesus (26:1-5) while an anonymous woman had tenderly anointed his body for burial (26:6-13). And at the end of the story, the dead Jesus is again surrounded by courageous discipleship and persistent hostility. But now the ordeal of the passion was over and the full reward of trust in Jesus would be revealed.

VIII. Resurrection and Mission

None of the Gospels ends with the death of Jesus. Matthew, like Mark before him, concludes his story of Jesus with a triumphant proclamation of the resurrection (28:1-15) and with a decisive mission thrust to the community (28:16-20). Although the passion of Jesus is our focus, it is important to comment briefly on how the evangelist follows through as his story moves from death to victory.

In Matthew's case this resurrection proclamation is something of an "anticlimax." The dramatic events that exploded at the moment of Jesus' death had already announced the triumph of the Gospel. Jesus' obedient death was vindicated by God's actions in tearing the Temple veil in half and liberating the dead from their tombs (see 27:51-54). In describing that redemptive effect of Jesus' death, Matthew had portrayed the raised saints as coming out of their tombs and entering Jerusalem to appear to many (27:53). But to maintain the priority of Jesus' own resurrection appearances and their foundational impact on the church, the evangelist had to blunt his dramatic description with the qualifying phrase "after his [Jesus'] resurrection" (27:53). In effect the holy ones had to linger in their tombs until Jesus himself was raised! Evidently, Matthew's theology and the demands of his narrative are at cross purposes here.[152] But now with the passion story completed Matthew can return to the thread of his narrative and bring the Gospel to its finale.

As had been the case throughout the passion narrative, Matthew utilizes source material from Mark but stamps it with his own distinctive brand. In the case of the resurrection Mark provides only the story of the discovery of the empty tomb (Mk 16:1-8).[153] Matthew will add to that his own special traditions reporting an appearance of Jesus to the women at the tomb (28:9-10), the continued efforts of Jesus' opponents to counteract the announcement of resurrection (28:11-16), and the final appearance of Jesus to his disciples on a mountain in Galilee, with its climactic missionary commission (28:16-20).

Each of these segments of the narrative continue the characteristic pespective of Matthew's Gospel. The women who come to the tomb are the very ones who had faithfully stood by Jesus and had witnessed his death and burial (cf. 27:55-56, 61). At dawn on Sunday, after the Sabbath day, they come "to see the sepulchre" (28:1). In Mark's account they come to "anoint" Jesus (Mk 16:1), but Matthew has clearly stated that the woman in Bethany had anointed Jesus' body for burial at the beginning of the passion story (see above, 26:6-13).

The atmosphere at the tomb is suffused with the same apocalyptic drama that had swirled around the death of Jesus. In Mark's account the meaning of the now-empty tomb is given in muted tones by a "young man" who sits calmly on the rolled back stone (Mk 16:5). But in Matthew the reader is a participant in the drama. Another "earth-

---

[152] As we are suggesting, the resurrection of the saints is not to be taken as historical description but is a theological affirmation by Matthew, using the biblical background of the expected resurrection of the holy ones in the final days. Cf. above, pp. 144-47.

[153] On this cf. D. Senior, *The Passion of Jesus in the Gospel of Mark*, 135-37. Most interpreters of Mark consider 16:1-8 to be the original ending to the Gospel;

quake" erupts (28:2; compare 27:51) and an "Angel of the Lord" descends from heaven to roll back the stone sealing the tomb. This heavenly messenger appears like "lightning" and is robed in garments "white as snow"(28:3). At the sight of this apparition, the soldiers who guard the tomb (see above, 27:66) are "shaken" with fear and become as dead men.

These details, most of them typical of Jewish descriptions of the endtime, give Matthew's account an electric charge and reinforce the impression that from the moment of Jesus' obedient death the new and decisive age of salvation has begun.[154] The descent of the "Angel of the Lord" and the subsequent opening of the tomb and the consternation of Jesus' enemies (in the persons of the guards) continue to affirm the vindication of Jesus and the Father's acceptance of his son's obedient death.

What causes death-like terror for the enemies of Jesus will be a source of consummate joy for his followers. Just as in the beginning of the Gospel Joseph had been relieved of his anguish by an "Angel of the Lord" (see 1:20; 2:13, 19) so, too, these faithful followers of Jesus will have their consternation dissolved by a similar messenger. The Angel's message to the women proclaims the meaning of the empty tomb. The crucified Jesus whom the women seek is not in the tomb, a place of death. "He is risen, as he said" (28:6). The phrase, "as he said," is a peculiar emphasis of Matthew (contrast Mk 16:6) that throws the spotlight on Jesus' own confidence in his victory over death. Each of the passion predictions included a prediction of resurrection as well. And at the final Passover meal as well as in his response to the High Priest during the trial, Jesus had confidently proclaimed his victory (see 26:29, 64). Thus the words of the Angel subtly reassert and validate the prophetic knowledge that the Matthean Jesus had consistently demonstrated.[155]

the other endings were added later to bring Mark into harmony with the other Gospels by including accounts of appearances.

[154] Cf. the biblical references and literature cited above, p. 144.

[155] This "higher" christological portrayal is recognized as a characteristic of Matthew's Gospel in comparison to Mark; cf., for example, A. Descamps, "Rédaction et christologie dans le recit matthéen de la Passion," in M. Didier (ed.), *L'Evangile*

The Angel also gives the women a mission: they are to announce the resurrection to the disciples and to tell them to assemble in Galilee for an encounter with Jesus (28:7). Unlike Mark's rendition, this is not presented as a promise of Jesus. Mark's phrase "as he told you" (Mk 16:7) is not repeated by Matthew even though at the last supper Jesus had made such a promise (see 26:32; par. Mk 14:28). Matthew's account will not end on a note of promise but of fulfillment. The Angel's announcement ("Lo, I have told you") prepares for the two appearances that Matthew actually narrates.

The first of these is to the women as they leave the tomb in "fear and great joy" to give their message to the disciples (28:8). This appearance to the women is found only in Matthew's Gospel and displays some characteristics of his theology. First of all it rewards the fidelity of the women who had stood by the cross of Jesus (in glaring contrast to the other disciples who had fled). Their "fear and great joy " at the message of the Angel — typical, if paradoxical, reactions in the Bible to divine revelations — are capped by a personal encounter with the Risen Christ that precedes that of the "eleven" in Galilee (28:16).

Secondly this encounter with the Risen Christ as the women are on their missionary journey fits into a consistent motif of the Gospel. The Risen Christ is present with his community and especially with those who proclaim the Gospel (see, for example, 10:40; 28:20; also 18:20). Reassurance in the course of their mission is, in fact, the message given by the Risen Christ to the women. As they approach Jesus and offer him profound homage (reminiscent of the response of the disciples to Jesus' manifestation on the sea, 14:33), he calms their fear and reiterates the command of the heavenly messenger: "Do not be afraid; go and tell my brethren to go to Galilee and they will see me" (28:10). Jesus' promise of ultimate reconciliation with the disciples who failed him, first made in the context of the Passover meal (26:32), is now reaffirmed by the Crucified and Risen Christ. Jesus takes the initiative to be reconciled with his "brethren" just as he had taught his disciples to do on several occasions in the Gospel (see 5:23-24; 6:12, 14-15; 18:21-35).

The bizarre incident that follows continues Matthew's use of pointed contrasts between Jesus and his opponents. As the women leave on their mission to announce the Gospel, the soldiers who had guarded the tomb report their astounding experience to the chief priests (28:11-15). Once again Matthew emphasizes the bad faith of the leaders. The priests and elders assemble in council and buy off the guards, an incident with obvious parallels to the gathering that had begun the passion story. Then, too, the priests and the elders had "taken counsel together" on how to destroy Jesus (26:3-5), and had also used money to achieve their ends (26:14-15). They instruct the guards to say that while they slept the disciples came and stole the body of Jesus. They also promise to protect the soldiers if the report of their sleeping on duty should anger Pilate, a promise that rings hollow when one remembers the indifference of the leaders to Judas' plight (27:3-10).

Matthew's intent is clear. The story contrasts the good will of Jesus and his faithful followers with that of the Jewish leaders. It also attempts to refute a counter-explanation of the empty tomb that Matthew's church had no doubt encountered. Both "explanations" — the gospel proclamation and the suggestion that the disciples perpetrated a hoax — assume that the tomb was empty.

The Gospel ends with another unique Matthean scene that catches up major themes of the Gospel and projects them into the community's future mission (28:16-20).[156]

The "eleven" (note that Matthew has not forgotten the fate of Judas) apparently accept the message of the women and gather on a mountaintop in Galilee (in contrast to

---

[156] For overall discussions of this scene, cf. R. Fuller, *The Formation of the Resurrection Narratives* (Philadelphia: Fortress, 1980), 79-93; B. J. Hubbard, *The Matthean Redaction of a Primitive Apostolic Commissioning: An Exegesis of Matthew 28:16-20* (SBLDS 19; Missoula: Scholars Press, 1974); J. Kingsbury, "The Composition and Christology of Matt 28:16-20," *Journal of Biblical Literature* 93 (1974) 573-84.

Luke's version where the apostles consider the women's report "an idle tale" and do not believe them; see Lk 24:11, 22-24). When the disciples catch sight of Jesus they offer him homage, but with a curious and difficult phrase Matthew suggests that even now their faith is weak and hesitant. "But some doubted" is one possible translation; the text could also imply that at the very moment the disciples offer homage they (*all* of them) hesitate or "doubt." [157] Matthew used this same word in 14:31 when describing Peter's "little faith" as he walked on the turbulent waters. Even though Peter recognized Christ, the disciple "hesitated" or "doubted" because of his fear. That mixture of faith and fear or hesitation seems to be noted again by Matthew as the disciples are about to be sent on their great mission.

Jesus' own words serve to reassure and validate their discipleship, just as the appearance to the women had done in the previous scene (28:8-10). He comes to his disciples imbued with full authority as the exalted Son of God and as the victorious Son of Man. [158] This triumphant moment on the mountaintop seems to be a preview of the finale of all history when the Son of Man would come to judge the world (cf. 24:29-31), the same victory Jesus had predicted as he stood before Sanhedrin: "But I tell you, from this moment you will see the Son of Man seated at the right hand of Power, and coming on the clouds of heaven" (26:64). In the aura of the resurrection the community of Jesus has a foretaste of that final day.

Yet between that mountaintop triumph and the final consummation of history stands an age-long task: the proclamation of the Gospel and the gathering of God's people (24:14). Now that the New Age of resurrection has dawned, the mission of redemption is no longer confined to Israel (as it had been during Jesus' lifetime, cf. 10:15; 15:24) but

---

[157] Cf. I. Ellis, "But Some Doubted," *New Testament Studies* (1967-68) 574-80.; C. H. Giblin, "A Note on Doubt and Reassurance in Mt. 28:16-20," *Catholic Biblical Quarterly* 37 (1975) 68-75.

[158] Cf. J. Meier, "Two Disputed Questions in Matt 28:16-20," *Journal of Biblical Literature* 96 (1977) 407-24. Note, too, that Matthew here has Jesus "approach" the disciples; a word usually used to describe approach of others to Jesus (cf. above, p. 53).

opens up to all the world.[159]

The specific content of the mission catches up characteristic notes of Matthew's Gospel. The apostles are to "make disciples" of all nations, baptizing them and gathering them into the community, reflecting Matthew's strong ecclesial interest. They are to be taught to observe all that Jesus had commanded, an emphasis on teaching and good deeds typical of Matthew. And as they carry out this worldwide mission, the Risen Jesus will be "with them" until the close of the age (28:20). In the opening scenes of the Gospel the infant Jesus had been given the name "Emmanuel," God-is-with-us (1:23). The closing verse of Matthew reaffirms that basis of the community's confidence: the Crucified and Risen Jesus is with them as they move out into history to take up their universal mission.

For Matthew, therefore, the conclusion of the Gospel continues the story of triumph over death that was the heart of the passion.

---

[159] Viewing Jesus' death and resurrection as the beginning of the new age enables Matthew to reconcile a mission of the earthly Jesus that had been restricted to Israel in the old age (cf. 10:5; 15:24) with the universal mission of the church that now, in the new, resurrection age, had opened up to all nations (28:19). On this aspect of Matthew's mission theology, cf. D. Senior and C. Stuhlmueller, *The Biblical Foundations for Mission* (Maryknoll: Orbis, 1983), 238-41.

PART III
THE PASSION OF JESUS: MATTHEW'S MESSAGE

Having read carefully through Matthew's passion narrative it is time to take stock of Matthew's message. The passion brings to eloquent and dramatic expression some of the most fundamental motifs of Matthew's Gospel. As we have noted at several points in our study, the passion narrative invites the Christian reader to be involved in the drama — reflecting on the experience of the suffering Christ, walking in the shoes of the various characters (both good and bad), and probing one's own reactions to the crisis of suffering and death. At every turn the rich theology of Matthew's passion narrative provides openings for the reader to measure the depth of his or her discipleship.

I. The Passion and Matthew's Portrayal of Jesus

The major character of the passion story is, of course, Jesus. He alone suffers and dies, and around his words and actions turns the entire drama. Therefore Matthew's perspective is fundamentally christological. The significance of Jesus' suffering and death is viewed through the lens of Matthew's convictions about the ultimate identity of Jesus. The depth of those convictions leads Matthew to present a portrait of Jesus that seems to have a "higher" christology than that of Mark. In Matthew's account Jesus clearly foretells his fate and seems to stand even more at the center of each scene. Rather than describe this as a "higher" christology than that of Mark or Luke — thereby implying Matthew's Gospel is in some way more advanced or evolved than the other Synoptics — it may be preferable to say that Matthew's protrayal is simply *different* in tone from that of Mark. Each Gospel presents Jesus from the perspective of full resurrection faith.

We can summarize some of Matthew's characteristic portrayal of Jesus in the following statements.

> *Jesus is the obedient Son of God who fulfills the Scriptures and is faithful to God's will unto death.*

At its most basic level Matthew's passion story is a story of fidelity. As we noted earlier, Matthew portrays a Jesus fiercely committed to the cause of "fulfilling all justice" (3:15).[1] Despite the temptations of Satan (4:1-11) or the cold hostility of opponents or the hesitations of his disciples, the Matthean Jesus moves through his ministry with unwavering dedication to the way of justice.

The torturous way of the passion is no exception. While the opponents plot against him, Jesus reasserts his commitment unto death (26:1-5). When the Passover comes, Jesus proclaims the approach of his opportune moment, his *kairos* (26:18), when his obedience would be tested. Over the bread and the cup he reaffirms the spirit of his entire mission: the giving of his body and blood for the sake of the kingdom (26:26-29). While the disciples sleep Jesus prays repeatedly that God's will be done (26:36-46). At the moment of arrest Jesus refuses violence and tells his captors that the Scriptures must be fulfilled (26:47-56).

The trial scenes continue the thread. In vivid contrast to Peter who denies his discipleship, Jesus stands before the

---

[1]Cf. above, Part I, pp. 26-30.

hostile Sanhedrin and fearlessly accepts his role as the Christ and Son of God (26:57-75). And before Pilate Jesus stands silent and uncompromised as he is rejected by his own people and his fate sealed in death (27:11-26).

Matthew clearly makes this issue of "fidelity" a major motif of the concluding scenes of the passion. As he hangs on the cross Jesus is once more "tempted" by a procession of taunters: "If you are the Son of God, come down from the cross.." (27:40). "He trusts in God, let God deliver him now, if he desires him; for he said, 'I am the Son of God' "(27:43). But just as Jesus had rejected the attempts of Satan to turn him aside from the way of fidelity so Jesus' silent commitment to the cross turns back the taunts of his opponents. The prayer on Jesus' dying lips is Psalm 22, the great prayer of the Just One of Israel who tenaciously holds onto trust in Yahweh despite the assaults of his opponents. The Matthean Jesus dies in anguish but faithful to the spirit in which he lived: the final surge of life in his broken body is an act of obedience (27:50).

Matthew's portrayal is not intended simply to give a compelling example of faithfulness but is part of a larger canvas which conveys the unique identity of Jesus. Jesus' fidelity marks him as *the* Israelite, remaining true to God where Israel itself may have wavered. Jesus is *the* Son of God, the royal Messiah who is intimate with God and in total symmetry with God's will, a fidelity far excelling the bonds between God and any king of Israel. Jesus is *the* Just One bound as Son to Father with an intimacy and tenacity far exceeding any previous expression of piety. As such Jesus is the "fulfillment" of Israel's own dream expressed in the Scriptures. Matthew shades Jesus' entire life with the tones of scriptural fulfillment, not in a mechanistic sense of simply showing the correspondence between texts of the Bible and details of Jesus' life, but as a way of proclaiming that Jesus is indeed the longed-for redeemer of Israel and the ultimate expression of God's intended will for his people.

The proof of Jesus' fidelity and the final expression of his obedience to God's will is demonstrated in the passion. The

Gospel does not portray Jesus' commitment unto death as a fanatical quest for martyrdom or a morbid riveting on suffering and death. As the story unfolds it becomes clear that a primary cause of Jesus' death is the hostility of his opponents, a hostility generated by Jesus' own teaching and healing. Jesus is ultimately *put to death.* At the same time, however, the Gospel also presents the death of Jesus as inevitable, foreseen, and accepted. While human forces move to quench the life of Jesus, on another level that death is absorbed into the mysterious redemptive plan of God and transformed into a life-giving force. It is on this level that the Gospel portrays Jesus as the Son of Man committed to going to Jerusalem and offering his life in ransom for the many (see, for example, 20:17-19, 28). Acceptance of death becomes for the Matthean Jesus the acceptance of God's will to save humanity.

Jesus' fidelity in the passion demonstrates that every fiber of his being is in harmony with God. The Matthean Jesus indeed had come "not to destroy the law and the prophets but to fulfill them" (5:17); he is committed to "fulfill all justice." Such singular fidelity ultimately flows from the very identity of Jesus as the Son of God, the unique revealer of God to Israel and the world.

Jesus is the Christ and Servant of God whose redemptive mission comes to its final expression in the cross, which frees God's people from sin and death.

For Matthew the death of Jesus is not only the final revelation of his identity but the most powerful expression of his redemptive mission.

That the death of Jesus effects freedom from sin and death is powerfully presented in Matthew's passion story. The interpretive words over the bread and wine at the last Passover meal strongly assert this. The blood of Jesus is to be "poured out for many *for the forgiveness of sins"* (see 26:28). On the cross, Matthew's Jesus is mocked for having "saved others" but being unable to save himself (27:42). But the thunderous events that follow upon the death of Jesus belie that mockery. The cosmic signs demonstrate that indeed Jesus in death saved others: the earth is split and the tombs broken open and those asleep in death rise to new life (27:51-53). No other Gospel presents the salvific impact of Jesus' passion in such explicit terms. Through his obedient death Jesus triumphs over death and that breakthrough is extended to all of God's people. The saints who rise from their mortal sleep are the first generation of those given new life in Jesus' name.

As we have already traced in Part One, this emphasis on salvation is present from the first moment of Matthew's story.[2] Matthew explicitly identifies Jesus as the Christ, the royal Son of David, the one who would answer the longings of Israel for salvation.[3] The very name given to the infant Messiah bears salvific meaning: He is called Jesus "for he will save his people from their sins" (1:22). As Jesus begins his ministry in Galilee a quotation from Isaiah (9:1-2) stresses its redemptive meaning: "...the people who sat in darkness have seen a great light, and for those who sat in the region and shadow of death light has dawned" (4:16). The powerful ministry of teaching and healing that dominates chapters 5 through 15 of the Gospel illustrates the defeat of "death" in its many forms as the Matthean Jesus brings life to those in darkness. When John the Baptist asks if Jesus is "he who is to come" (11:3) he is reminded of the "deeds of the Christ": sight to the blind, mobility for the disabled, the cleansing of lepers, hearing for the deaf, resurrection for the dead, and good news for the poor (11:2-6).

That liberating ministry prompts Matthew to designate Jesus as fulfilling the words of Isaiah concerning the Servant of God who "took our infirmities and bore our diseases" (8:17, quoting Is 53:4). After another burst of healing activity Matthew again applies the Servant image to Jesus, this time stressing his humility and gentleness as he "proclaims justice to the Gentiles" (12:18-21, citing Is 42:1-4).

[2]Cf. especially, Part I, pp. 18-23.

[3]The genealogy which begins Matthew's Gospel explicitly identifies Jesus as "Son of David" (1:1) and as the "Christ" (1:16, 17).

Jesus the Servant is also the "Son of Man" who came "not to be served but to serve, and to give his life as a ransom for many" (20:28). Although subtly drawn, Matthew does portray Jesus as this Servant in the passion story as he stands silent before his accusers (26:62-63; 27:12-14), is tortured and mocked for his supposed claims to power (26:67-68; 27:27-31).

Matthew presents Jesus' death on Golgotha, therefore, not as a tragic anomaly but as the final and definitive expression of a life poured out in teaching, healing, and solidarity with those in need. The death of Jesus is redemptive because his entire life and mission are redemptive.

This portrayal of Jesus and his mission not only reaffirms the foundation of the community's hope as a redeemed people but also presents the ultimate model of all Christian mission. The one who follows Jesus is to follow him in the "way of justice," finding life in the giving of life.

Jesus is the Son of Man who goes the way of humiliation and death but will come in triumph at the end of time.

Matthew's passion narrative had opened with Jesus' prediction that the "Son of Man will be delivered up to be crucified" (26:2). That reference to the "Son of Man's" humiliation ties into the passion story a thread that had been woven throughout much of the Gospel. The Son of Man who would come in glory at the end of time to judge all humanity would first experience humiliation, defeat, and death.[4] The passion charts with brutal realism the "defeat" of the Son of Man. He is betrayed and deserted by his friends (cf. the title's explicit use in 26:24, 45), delivered to his enemies, and dies in desolation: events explicitly foretold in Jesus' predictions about the Son of Man's fate.

Paradoxically, the passion story is also the beginning of the Son of Man's triumph. Standing as a seemingly defenseless prisoner before the Sanhedrin, Jesus boldly makes that

[4]This is the assertion of the passion predications (cf. 16:21; 18:22-23; 20:17-19).

claim to Caiaphas, the High Priest: "But I tell you, you will see the Son of Man seated at the right hand of Power, and coming on the clouds of heaven" (26:64). That claim seems empty to the opponents of Jesus within the passion story. He is subsequently mocked, condemned, and executed. But the Christian reader catches the deep irony so often at work in the narrative. Jesus' claim to victory is validated in the very manner of his dying. Through death he finds life, affirming his own teaching to his disciples: "For whoever would save his life will lose it..." (16:25).

Demonstration of that new life comes in the way Matthew portrays the events that immediately follow Jesus' death. Divine power tears open the Temple veil, shatters the earth and frees those trapped in the tombs (27:51-53). When the women come to the tomb, they again encounter a shaking of the earth and an Angel of the Lord who comes in brilliant array to roll back the stone and to announce the Son of Man's victory over death (28:1-7). All of these are signs expected for the endtime but they happen now in the wake of Jesus' humiliation and death to show that this was a death like no other. It is the dying and rising of the victorious Son of Man. The final scene of the Gospel presents the coming of the Son of Man, imbued with full authority, as he dispatches the community on its mission (28:16-20).

The dark tones of the passion story and the continuing opposition to Jesus beyond the grave (see 27:62-66; 28:11-15) insure the paradoxical nature of the Son of Man's triumph. What appears as weakness and failure from a purely human perspective is recognized as authentic power from the perspective of faith.[5] This clash of perspectives runs throughout the passion but comes to its most explicit statement as Jesus is mocked by the Sanhedrin (26:67-68), the Roman cohort (27:27-32), and those present on Golgotha (27:38-44). Jesus' claims to have divine authority as the Christ, the Son of God, the Son of Man, or as Prophet are derided. But the reader understands that ultimately it is not

---

[5]This is an important part of Mark's theology carried over into Matthew; cf. D. Senior, *The Passion of Jesus in the Gospel of Mark*, 144-48.

Jesus but his opponents and their values which are on trial. The signs of power — the royal mantle, the crown, the sceptre, the acts of homage — meant to deride Jesus are themselves mocked because the Gospel reveals that authentic greatness is not to be found in these symbols of oppressive power but in the way of self-transcendence and service, the way of the Son of Man (see, for example, 20:25-28). The power of those who bring Jesus to death — the Sanhedrin, the Romans — is revealed as bankrupt, even as they taunt Jesus to save himself from crucifixion. The reader knows that in that cross will be exercised the very power of God over death.

Thus one of the most profound and challenging motifs of the passion story is its statement about the exercise of power. Power used to exploit and oppress is unmasked as ultimately impotent. The power that comes from giving life is God's power and is ultimately redemptive.

In the crisis of suffering and death Jesus is the exemplar of authentic faith.

One of the recurrent motifs of Matthew's Gospel is the insistence on integrity.[6] Authentic discipleship is characterized by deeds that match words (see, for example 7:21-28; 20:28-32, etc.). "Hypocrisy," a capital sin in this Gospel, is precisely the failure to do what one believes or teaches (cf. 23:2-7). Jesus is presented by Matthew as the ultimate exemplar of true fidelity or "righteousness." That is especially true in the passion where the crucible of suffering and death becomes the final test of one's deepest values.

Throughout the narrative we have noted places where Matthew has blended into the scenes echoes of Jesus' earlier teachings. Thus in the garden as his hour of crisis approaches Jesus is alert, watching for the coming of the *kairos* and praying in words that echo his own instruction on prayer in the Sermon on the Mount (see 26:39, 42 and 6:9-13) and in his apocalyptic discourse (24:42-44). At the

6Cf. above, Part One, p. 36.

moment of the arrest (26:52-54) Jesus refuses to use arms in his defense and tempers the violence of his followers just as he had taught in the Sermon on the Mount (5:38-42, 43-48). His faith and courage throughout the interrogations and torture inflicted by the Sanhedrin and Pilate incarnate the attitudes Jesus encouraged in his disciples as he sent them out on their mission of justice (10:16-20). As he stares death in the face (27:45-50), Jesus places his entire being in the hands of his God, praying the psalm that gives final expression to the unconditional trust that characterizes Jesus from the first moment of his public ministry.

The Jesus of Matthew's Gospel is, therefore, the authentic portrait of the Christian before the mystery of death. Death thrusts its way into Jesus' life early in the Gospel as he himself experiences the "persecution for justice's sake" that he had warned would be the lot of those who proclaim the rule of God (5:10-11). And when that persecution mounts to the terror of arrest and death, Jesus' faith in God is tested to the full. Jesus is *the* believer, the child of God before the specter of death. Matthew does not portray that face-to-face encounter in ideal terms. Jesus' final prayer is a prayer of anguish and near-despair as in the web of death he experiences the absence of God. All other supports and all relationships seem stripped away; only the handhold of God's fidelity seems left as Jesus dies with the anguished lament of Psalm 22, the prayer of the beleagured believer, on his lips. The realism of Matthew's portrayal allows Christians of all ages to recognize their own struggle with mortality and death. Christian death need not be placid and fable-like to be authentically Christian. The hoarse tones of the lament are the sounds of a genuine relationship with God. In the very struggle to trust, genuine faith can be expressed. The anguish of death itself can be a prayer for a child of God.

The final word of the Gospel is, of course, that such trust is not in vain. The relationship with God upon which all of Jesus' hopes were based did not prove illusory. Through that very trust Jesus' cause was vindicated and his own body and spirit given new life, a destiny offered to all who follow in the way of justice.

II. The Crisis of the Passion and Response to the Gospel

Human character is often laid bare in the arena of suffering and death. Crisis can be the proving ground of the values upon which choices are actually made. The dramatic force of the passion story surely illustrates this. Strengths or weaknesses only latent or barely breaking the surface in earlier parts of the Gospel explode into view in the tense reality of the passion. Undoubtedly this was part of the intent of the passion story as proclaimed in the community. The readers are invited to take their own places in the drama and to see how they might respond to those decisive moments when God's grace knifes unexpectedly into the texture of human history.

The Crisis of the passion reveals disciples of "Little Faith."

Mark's presentation of the disciples in the passion is noted for its emphasis on their stark failure.[7] Matthew's account is almost identical. Only the wider context of Matthew's Gospel, wherein the disciples are portrayed as having "little faith" in contrast to Mark where they often evidence "no faith," tends to mute the negative portrayal of the disciples in this Gospel.

Matthew's passion story seems to grind inexorably toward the disciples' abject failure. In the opening scenes of the narrative we see all of them object to the woman who attempts to anoint Jesus (26:8),[8] and one of them goes to the chief priests to barter for Jesus' betrayal (26:14-16). The final Passover is surrounded by Jesus' predictions of treachery by Judas and desertion and denial by the rest of the disciples (26:20-25, 30-35). In Gethsemane the disciples do not "watch and pray" as Jesus asks but fall asleep at the

---

[7]Cf. D. Senior, *The Passion of Jesus in the Gospel of Mark*, 148-50.

[8]Note that the identification of the complainers as "disciples" by Matthew is one of those infrequent instances when his portrayal of the disciples is even more negative than Mark's (cf. Mark 14:4 who says only that "some" were indignant at the woman, without identifying the complainers as disciples).

moment of greatest crisis (26:36-46) and therefore prove unprepared and cowardly when the enemies of Jesus come to arrest him. They display betrayal of their call as one of them retaliates with a sword — in direct contradiction to Jesus' teachings — and when all of them abandon Jesus and flee in panic (26:47-56). Peter follows at a distance but his shaky bravado soon collapses as he denies his discipleship with an oath at the very moment Jesus stands on trial before the Sanhedrin (26:69-75).

In Matthew's story, as in Mark's, all of those disciples explicitly chosen and entrusted with his mission abandon Jesus and betray their discipleship in the crisis of the passion. Matthew's special interest in Judas even adds to this abject picture. Whenever Judas is on the scene Matthew gives close attention to this personification of discipleship failure. In Judas' own words we discover that lust for money motivates his betrayal (26:15). Again in words found only in Matthew, Judas seems to condemn himself by responding to Jesus at the supper, "Is it I, Rabbi?" (26:25), words that plainly contrast with the more reverent and fearful question of the other disciples. At the moment of the arrest Judas again speaks with Jesus, his words of greeting and his kiss a blasphemous contradiction to his act of treachery (26:50). The awful finale is Judas' own suicide when his alliance with the opponents of Jesus proves futile and he chooses death rather than repentance (27:3-10).

Matthew's haunting portrayal of Judas probes the ultimate consequences of betraying the call to follow Jesus. To do so not only leads to deception and dishonesty but to death itself.

However, the stark tones of Matthew's reflection on the failure of the disciples are tempered by the full framework of the Gospel. When the whole story is taken into account we learn that the fate of the eleven who did not choose death is reconciliation with Jesus and renewal of their call to discipleship and mission (28:16-20). The full span of the Gospel prepares the reader both for the disciples' failures as well as their ultimate fidelity. A favored term of Matthew that captures this mixed portrayal of the disciples is "little faith."[9] The disciples loyally follow Jesus (4:22), are entrusted with his mission (10:1-8), prove "understanding" of his teaching (13:11, 51-52; 16:12), and boldly acclaim him as "Son of God" (14:33). But in crisis they prove hesitant and fearful. Peter exemplifies this mixed image in the Matthean version of the walking on the water. The leader of the disciples is able to share in Jesus' divine power over the chaos of the sea but becomes "hesitant" and "fearful" when he senses the force of the storm. Jesus brands this "little faith" (see 14:31).

Evidence of this "mixed" image can be found even in the tragic events of the passion. With the exception of Judas, the disciples are evidently on Jesus' side — a bond that Matthew stresses in the early part of the passion story. They obediently prepare the Passover meal (26:17-19) and are genuinely distressed at Jesus' predictions of betrayal, addressing him as "Lord" (26:22). And even as Jesus foretells their failure he also proclaims that in the triumph of resurrection he will go before them to Galilee, the place where their discipleship will be renewed (26:30-32). Even Peter's vehement denials are tempered by his tears of remorse (26:75, Matthew adds that Peter wept "bitterly") and by the stark contrast between his fate and that of Judas. The reader of Matthew knows that this flawed disciple is both the "rock" upon which the church of Jesus is to be built and the "scandal" or stumbling rock attempting to impede Jesus (16:18, 23 — both are Matthean additions).

The concluding scene of the Gospel reaffirms this realistic portrayal of the disciples. Even in the glow of the resurrection and at the climactic moment of the Risen Jesus' appearance to his community, Matthew describes the eleven as "hesitating" (28:17). The number "eleven" recalls the tragedy of Judas, and the hesitancy of the disciples reminds the readers that "little faith" is a recurring condition of Christian existence, especially when confronted with its mission in the world.

[9]Cf. above Part One, p. 44-45.

Through the passion story Matthew is able to remind his community that the brutal realities of persecution, suffering, and death are conditions where discipleship is most severely tested and where "little faith" and the failure to be alert and prayerful can lead not only to the possibility of cowardice and flight but even to the destruction of the bond between Jesus and his followers.

The Crisis of the passion reveals "unexpected" disciples who respond with generosity and courage.

There is another set of characters in Matthew's narrative that serve to instruct the community on the meaning of discipleship. There are minor, often one-scene characters, who may not bear the explicit designation "disciple" or "apostle" but, in fact, exemplify the traits of authentic followers of Jesus.

The anonymous woman who anoints Jesus at Bethany is a prime example (26:6-13). Her act of homage to Jesus and her awareness of his approaching death are put in direct contrast to the disciples who protest her generosity, despite the fact that Jesus has just instructed them on the imminence of his death. In defense of the woman Jesus calls her action "a beautiful work" (26:10) and predicts it will become part of the community's world-wide proclamation (26:13).

Another woman, Pilate's wife, steps briefly into the passion drama but shows unexpected devotion to Jesus (27:19). She has been warned in a dream about Jesus' innocence and, like Joseph in the infancy narrative, she acts on that dream by counseling Pilate not to condemn that "just man." The guards who execute Jesus and who keep vigil on Golgotha are another unexpected example of discipleship. Having witnessed the awesome portents that erupt at the moment Jesus dies, the centurion and his companions are moved to confess Jesus as Son of God (27:54). By expanding the number from a single soldier (see Mk 15:39) to many and by aligning them with the faithful women who are also present at the cross (27:55-56) Matthew seems to portray these witnesses as the first gathering of the community in the wake of Jesus' triumph over death. This mixture of Jews and Gentiles is a preview of the *ekklesia* to be formed in Jesus' name. The essential reality of the church is participating in the death and resurrection of Jesus.

Matthew gives special attention to the women of this new community. From those present on Golgotha, two — Mary Magdalene and the "other Mary" (presumably Mary the mother of the sons of Zebedee mentioned in 27:56) — will be present at the burial (27:61) and become the first to discover the empty tomb (28:1). Matthew's choice of two may reflect the emphasis on two witnesses needed for major issues in Jewish tradition.[10] These are not mere figurines in the scene. The evangelist draws a straight line from the women's faithful presence at the cross through their witness to the burial and their discovery of the empty tomb into their commissioning as the first to proclaim the resurrection to the rest of the disciples (28:7). Their faithful presence stands in evident contrast not only with the absence of the other disciples but with the hostile and deceptive presence of the guard arranged by the opponents of Jesus (see 27:62-66; 28:11-15). The importance of the women's role and mission is underlined by Matthew's unique presentation of their encounter with the Risen Jesus (28:9-10). In Matthew's Gospel this is the first resurrection appearance and its purpose is to validate the mission given to the women by the Angel at the tomb.

In Matthew's account, therefore, the women who persevere through the passion are the first entrusted with the community's mission and become the vehicles of reconciliation between the Risen Jesus and the eleven.

A final character in the cast of "hidden disciples" is Joseph of Arimathea (27:57-61). His discipleship is also displayed by solidarity with the crucified Jesus, in contrast to the neglect of the other disciples. The fact that Joseph is

---

[10]Cf. Dt. 19:15; Matthew seems to be conscious of this in 18:16 (a charge against a member of the community must be confirmed by two or three witnesses) and 26:60 (two witnesses come forward to accuse Jesus of threats against the Temple).

"rich" and yet willing to risk his possessions by being identified with someone publicly discredited and executed is an obvious lesson for members of Matthew's community.

The device of using minor characters as examples of authentic response to the Gospel, often in contrast with the flawed or failed response of more central figures on the scene, is something Matthew has employed throughout his Gospel: the homage of the Gentile magi in contrast to the hostility of Herod and his Jerusalem court (2:1-18), the bold faith of the centurion in contrast to the faith of Israel (8:5-13), the tenacious quest of the Canaanite woman to share in Jesus' mission while the Pharisees attack him over points of the law (15:21-28; 15:1-20), the openness of outcasts and sinners to Jesus in contrast to the hostility of the leaders (11:11-16; 2:28-32). These are some instances where Matthew uses these "counter-examples" to drive home the meaning of discipleship.

The fact that these examples come from more marginal or unexpected sources is an effective dramatic ploy that also, in itself, proclaims a profound aspect of the Gospel, one emphasized by Matthew: the self-proclaimed insiders can miss the moment of grace while those dismissed as unlikely can prove more open.[11] In the passion story such contrasts are pushed to their furthest point, with "outsiders" remaining faithful and Jesus' designated disciples, along with his opponents, failing to respond to grace.

The passion is the summit of the deadly hostility of Jesus' opponents and reveals the tragedy of their failure.

In Part One we noted that Matthew's Gospel stresses the opposition that Jesus and his message encounter.[12] That

---

[11] This note of "reversal" comes through in several passages of Matthew's Gospel; see, for example, 8:11-12 (the Gentiles will eat at table with Abraham, Isaac, and Jacob in the kingdom of heaven while the "sons of the kingdom" will be cast outside); 11:20-24 (it will go better for the pagan and sinful towns of Tyre, Sidon, and Sodom than it will for the Galilean villages of Chorazin, Bethsaida, and Capernaum); 21:32 (the tax collectors and harlots will go into the kingdom of God before the chief priests and elders).

[12] Cf. above, Part I, pp. 26-33, 36-37.

opposition begins with the very rumor of his birth, extends throughout his public ministry, and comes to its climax in his passion and death. Those opposed to Jesus are generally the Jewish leaders; during his public ministry these are often grouped by Matthew as the "scribes and Pharisees," and in the setting of Jerusalem and the passion story, the "chief priests and elders."[13] In the passion narrative the leaders manage to widen the circle of opposition. They persuade the "crowds," who up to this point have been generally neutral and often favorable to Jesus, to turn against him, and Pilate, too, becomes a reluctant instrument of their will. At the decisive moment of the condemnation of Jesus Matthew has the "entire people" call for Jesus' crucifixion (27:25).

Because this part of the passion story has been so abused in the cause of anti-semitism and also because it was undoubtedly important for the evangelist, we must weigh its overall meaning carefully. As already suggested, the opposition to Jesus has several levels of meaning in this Gospel. The alienation between Jesus and many of the Jewish leaders has a basis in history, not only in the conflicts between Jesus and some of his contemporaries who found his message offensive, but also in the mounting tension between early Christianity and Pharisaic Judaism which had an influence on Matthew's Gospel.[14]

In addition the opponents take their place among a whole cast of characters and events in the Gospel which shape Matthew's message. That is, they have a rhetorical or literary function, meant to influence the reader's understanding of the Gospel message. As such the opponents fall under the heading of "response to the Gospel" that we are now considering.

The Jewish leaders seem to have a one-dimensional role

---

[13]Matthew refers to the "scribes and Pharisees" ten times, most of them in passages special to him (cf., for example, 5:20; 12:38; 15:1; 23:2, 13, 14, 15, 34). The grouping "chief priests and elders" is found mainly in the passion story (cf. 26:3, 47; 27:1, 3, 12, 20, 41). Cf. further, A. Klijn, "Scribes, Pharisees, Highpriests and Elders in the New Testament," *Novum Testamentum* 3 (1959) 259-67; S. Van Tilborg, *The Jewish Leaders in Matthew* (Leiden: Brill, 1972).

[14]Cf. our discussion of this above, pp. 12-13, 34-35.

in Matthew: they exemplify those who are aggressively closed to the Gospel and thereby fail to respond to the grace God offers. The passion story demonstrates the deadly outcome of such a closed-minded stance. In the opening scene the leaders are presented as plotting in secret against Jesus' life, bringing to term the hostility mounted against him since the beginning of the Gospel (26:3-5). They barter with Judas the betrayer (26:14-16) and are the agents for Jesus' arrest (26:47). Later Matthew shows that even their alliance with Judas turns sour as the leaders coldly reject his attempt at restitution (27:3-10). When they finally have Jesus in their control they seek false witness against him (26:59), and after rejecting his claim to be the Messiah they themselves taunt and abuse their prisoner (26:67-68). During the Roman trial their role continues, as they persuade the Roman Governor and the crowds to release Barabbas and crucify Jesus (27:11-26). On Golgotha they mock the crucified Jesus (27:41-43). And, in a touch found only in Matthew, their opposition continues beyond Jesus' death, as "the chief priests and Pharisees" demand a guard at the tomb (27:62-66) and then bribe the soldiers to spread a false report when events turn out differently than they expect (28:11-15).

There is no relief in Matthew's portrayal; the leaders remain one-dimensional in their rejection of Jesus. From the standpoint of the Gospel they are people who have completely missed the *kairos*, the moment of opportune grace. Like the foolish people in the days of Noah, or the wicked servant, or the imprudent virgins, or the person of one talent —all characters of Matthew's parables in the apocalyptic discourse (24:36-25:30) — the leaders are destined for judgment because they were found badly wanting at the advent of the kingdom.

It must be admitted that by this means the evangelist and his community vent their hostile feelings toward Pharisaic Judaism. The synagogue's rejection of the Christian mission is seen as tantamount to rejection of Jesus, God's Messiah, and Matthew seems convinced that for such rejection his contemporaries will experience judgment, just as the characters in Jesus' parables do. As we have suggested in our discussion of the passion story, Matthew may also interpret the agonies of the Jewish revolt against Rome and the subsequent destruction of the Jerusalem Temple in A. D. 70 as signs of God's judgment for the sin of rejection.[15]

This aspect of Matthew's theology bears a heavy burden, as the history of Christianity demonstrates. Too easily Matthew's theological interpretation of events in his time (the Jewish revolt and the destruction of the Temple), which the evangelist saw as divine punishment for the generation that had rejected Jesus and the Gospel, when read in a different age and now as part of a sacred, normative text, can be interpreted as divine judgment on an entire people and for all time. This later brand of anti-semitism would be inconceivable for an evangelist and a religious community who themselves were of strong Jewish origin. But the potential for later misreading is there in Matthew's portrayal of the Jewish leaders and, tragically, the potential has been realized.[16] No part of the Gospel has been more abused in this fashion than Matthew's passion narrative, especially the climactic verse in which the entire people reject Jesus and accept responsibility for his blood (cf. our discussion of 27:24-25).

Modern interpreters of the Gospel, whether they be teachers, preachers, liturgists, or parents with their children, have a responsibility to cushion such texts with wider understanding of the historical and social context of Matthew's Gospel and its struggle with Pharisaic Judaism. Such a context can go a long way to offsetting the mean potential of an anti-Jewish reading of the story.

But what we are calling the literary or rhetorical purpose of the characters in the Gospel should also be taken into account. Matthew's Gospel, after all, was not written to directly confront the Jewish communities of his time. Nor was it written primarily to arm his Christians against their Jewish opponents. The overall thrust of the Gospel is directed to the Christians and *their* response to the Gospel.

[15]Cf. above, pp. 116-22.

[16]Cf. the literature cited above in our discussion of 27:24-25, p. 116, n. 100.

All of the characters in the narrative — Jesus, the crowds, the disciples, the opponents — are potential reference points for the reader. All of these characters are in a sense "anachronistic" in that none of them are "contemporaries" of the reader. Just as the disciples are not characters drawn directly from Matthew's church but depict the first followers of Jesus, so the opponents of Jesus in the Gospel story are not the same as the leaders of the Pharisaic synagogues with whom Matthew's Christians may have been in conflict.

Therefore the reader is implicitly asked to scrutinize the attitudes, reactions, and activities of *each* character in the drama and to find played out there the full scope of Christian existence. If this be the case, then the primary identification of the opponents in Matthew's Gospel are not people outside the community, such as the leaders of Pharisaic Judaism, but Christians *inside* the community whose values betray them as opposed to Jesus and his message. Through the passion story Matthew illustrates the final end of those whose position places them at prominent places in the family of God but whose lack of integrity leads them to deny, oppose, and ultimately attempt to destroy the Gospel of God. Such a stance, in the very name of religious purity, is the ultimate blasphemy and brings with it its own judgment. Rather than use Matthew's portrayal of Jesus' opponents to falsely condemn the Jewish people (itself a betrayal of the Gospel) Christians should first turn the spotlight on themselves and ask if the attitudes of those who rejected and killed Jesus finds an echo in their own response to the Christian message.

III. The Passion and Matthew's Theology of History

Another deep current of Matthew's theology cresting in the passion narrative is the conviction that the person and mission of Jesus have definitive consequences for the history of salvation.[17] Because the death and resurrection of

---

[17]Cf. our discussion of this motif in Part I, pp. 38-40.

Jesus are perceived as the culmination of his mission it is not surprising that Matthew's theology of history is strongly present at this point in the Gospel.

From the start of the passion narrative "timing" is in evidence as Jesus predicts that his own "handing over" will coincide with the Passover, the great Jewish feast of liberation and future hope (26:1-2). Preparations to celebrate the Passover begin with Jesus' solemn words: "My *kairos* is at hand" (26:18), a statement that explicitly links the passion of Jesus with the awaited New Age when salvation would come.[18] And at the Last Supper Jesus interprets his impending death as a new covenant for the "forgiveness of sins" (26:28) and proclaims he will drink wine with his disciples "in my Father's kingdom" (26:29), both declarations bold announcements of the final days.

Matthew (following the lead of Mark) also presents Jesus' prayer in Gethsemane as an "eschatological" prayer, that is, as part of the final struggle in which evil is defeated and God's victory breaks into the world. Jesus exhorts his disciples to be "watchful" (26:38, 41), the needed stance for the coming of the day of the Lord (24:42-44), and his own prayer (26:39, 42) echoes the one he had taught his disciples in the Sermon on the Mount, a prayer for the coming of God's final rule (6:9-13). The arrival of Judas and the armed mob is the signal that for Jesus the eschatological moment had come (26:45-46). In the stillpoint of the passion Jesus would experience that decisive struggle with evil which the community would encounter diffused throughout history. In the light of Jesus' victory over evil and death, the community's own ultimate destiny is made clear.

Even as the nightmare of the passion seems to deepen, the Gospel's victorious perspective makes itself felt. Standing helpless before the Sanhedrin Jesus answers the High Priest's question by affirming that the eschatological triumph of the Son of Man will be seen even now (26:64). And as the final darkness entwines the cross (27:45) and Jesus prays his death prayer, overwhelming signs of the New

---

[18]Cf. the eschatological significance of the word "*kairos*" above, pp. 60-61.

Age break across the landscape: the veil is split, the earth trembles, the tombs open, and the dead are raised (27:51-53). The resulting confession of Jesus as the "Son of God" by the centurion and his fellow soldiers and the presence of the faithful remnant near the cross are the first human signs of the triumph, as God's people begin to gather (27:54-56). As we have noted, Matthew's presentation of the discovery of the empty tomb (28:1-10) and the final reunion of the Risen Jesus with his community on the mountain in Galilee (28:16-20) continue this triumphant mode.

For Matthew's Gospel, therefore, even though the "close of the age" awaits realization (28:20), history has already turned on its axis from the age of sin and death to the age of forgiveness and new life. That view of human destiny was already announced in the story of Israel and its covenant. Jesus, as the fulfillment of the promises of Scripture, validates that view and brings it to actualization. The ultimate basis of Matthew's salvation history perspective is christological. Because he views Jesus as the Christ and as the Son of God whose perfect obedience reveals God's salvific will for the world, Jesus' fate must have ultimate significance for human history. The epicenter of Jesus' mission and the most penetrating revelation of his identity is his death for the many, and so it is at the moment of Jesus' passion that the turning point of history is most manifest.

As is the case with almost every aspect of Matthew's theology, such theological reflection is not purely speculative. The patterns of sacred history hold lessons for God's people.

It is not without significance that the New Age makes its entry at a moment of suffering and death. As we suggested earlier, Matthew finds this paradoxical pattern in the history of Israel as well as in the history of Jesus, and reaffirms it as the destiny of the post-resurrection community.[19] For some of the characters in the Gospel suffering and death come as judgment on their sinfulness. As illustrated in the fate of the wicked tenants in Jesus' parable, rejection and

---

[19]Cf. above, p. 43.

killing of the Son will bring their own retribution (Mt 21:40-43). Those who reject the Gospel and embrace evil — as exemplified by Jesus' opponents — will be left with nothing more than the death they choose. But for others the experience of suffering and death are not the wages or symptoms of sin but a purifying moment in which new life and new hope are enkindled. Jesus himself is the primary exemplar of this redemptive process. Through his death he enters into new life. The same destiny is promised for his disciples.

But it is important to note that Matthew reflects not only on the drama of individual and personal confrontation with death. The evangelist clearly sees the death and resurrection of Jesus as a turning point for the *community* of Israel as such. Some in that community would experience judgment. But the vineyard of Israel itself would continue in a new form, as the horizons of salvation are pushed open to all peoples willing to respond to the advent of grace.

Therefore the death-resurrection pattern of history would apply to the Christian community, too. In those moments when death seemed to threaten, Matthew reminds his community that in such discontinuity the grace of a New Age was present. Such moments of death had already come to Matthew's church in the relative failure of their mission to Israel and in the difficult changes imposed on the community through the influx of Gentiles. By viewing the pains of history through the lens of the passion, Matthew sought to embolden his church for its future. The Risen Jesus lived within the church. His passion now became the passion of the church; death remained a reality but now, in the light of the cross, could be confronted as a way to new life.

These central themes certify that the passion was not a foreboding chapter of Jesus' story from which Matthew and his community preferred to avert their glance. The realities of suffering, rejection, and death itself are squarely faced, and because of faith in Jesus made an integral, even central, part of the Good News.

SUBJECT INDEX

AUTHOR INDEX

SCRIPTURE INDEX